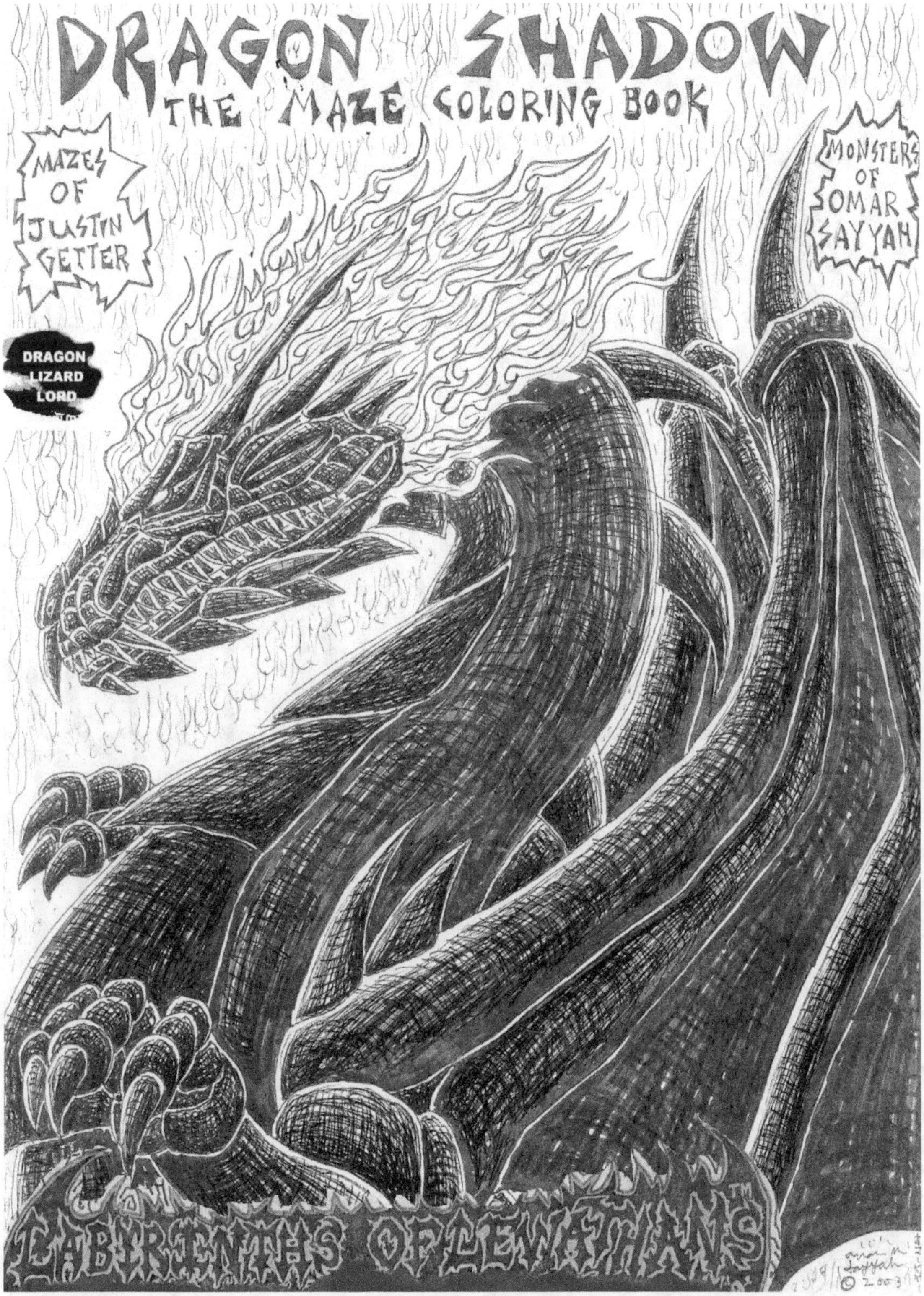

DRAGON SHADOW
THE MAZE COLORING BOOK

MAZES
OF
JUSTIN
GETTER

MONSTERS
OF
OMAR
SAYYAH

DRAGON
LIZARD
LORD

LABIRENTHS OF LEVIATHANS ™

© 2003

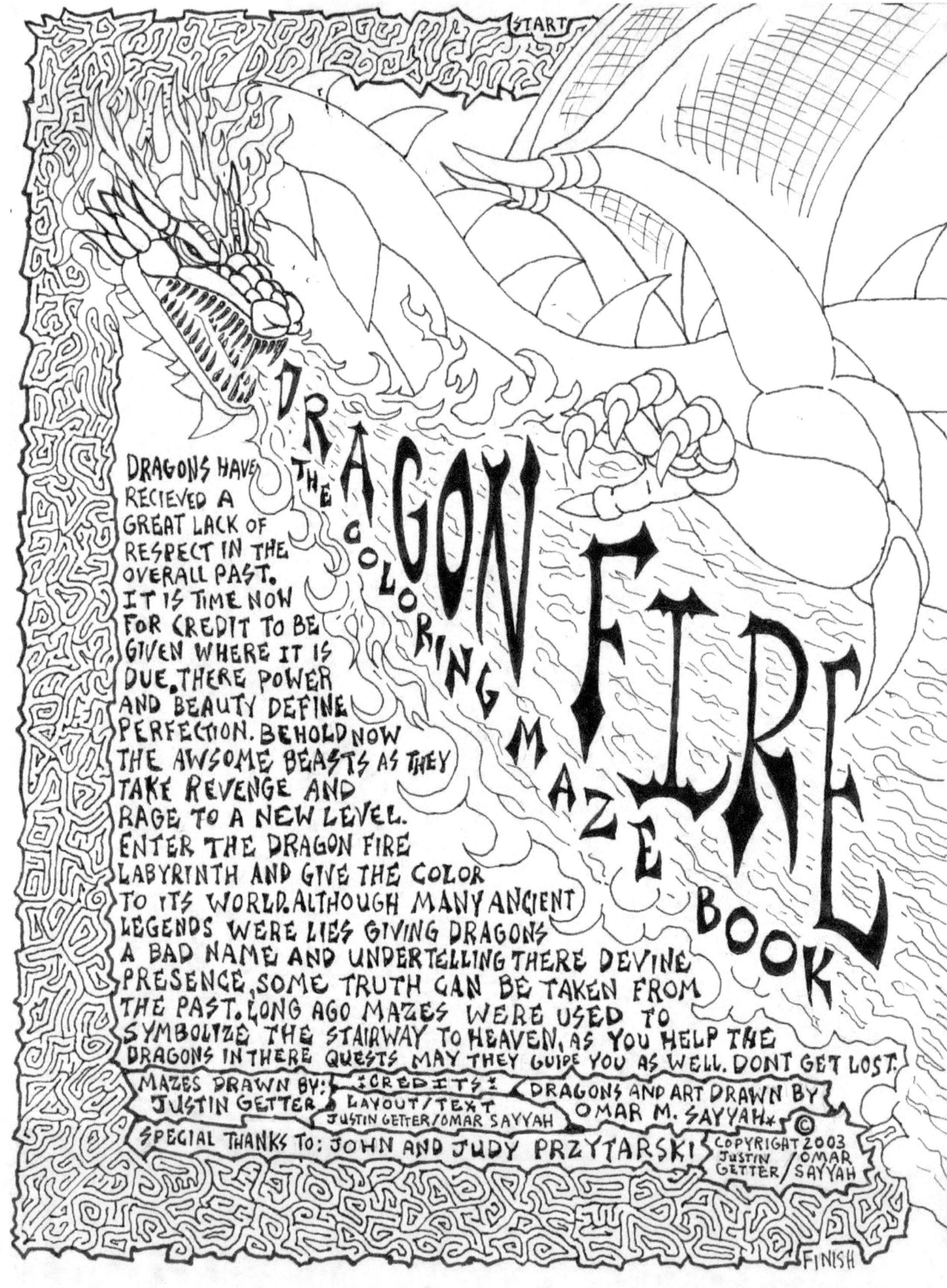

START

DRAGON FIRE
THE COLORING MAZE BOOK

DRAGONS HAVE RECIEVED A GREAT LACK OF RESPECT IN THE OVERALL PAST. IT IS TIME NOW FOR CREDIT TO BE GIVEN WHERE IT IS DUE. THERE POWER AND BEAUTY DEFINE PERFECTION. BEHOLD NOW THE AWSOME BEASTS AS THEY TAKE REVENGE AND RAGE TO A NEW LEVEL. ENTER THE DRAGON FIRE LABYRINTH AND GIVE THE COLOR TO ITS WORLD. ALTHOUGH MANY ANCIENT LEGENDS WERE LIES GIVING DRAGONS A BAD NAME AND UNDERTELLING THERE DEVINE PRESENCE, SOME TRUTH CAN BE TAKEN FROM THE PAST. LONG AGO MAZES WERE USED TO SYMBOLIZE THE STAIRWAY TO HEAVEN, AS YOU HELP THE DRAGONS IN THERE QUESTS MAY THEY GUIDE YOU AS WELL. DONT GET LOST.

CREDITS

MAZES DRAWN BY: JUSTIN GETTER

LAYOUT/TEXT JUSTIN GETTER/OMAR SAYYAH

DRAGONS AND ART DRAWN BY OMAR M. SAYYAH* ©

SPECIAL THANKS TO: JOHN AND JUDY PRZYTARSKI

COPYRIGHT 2003 JUSTIN /OMAR GETTER / SAYYAH

FINISH

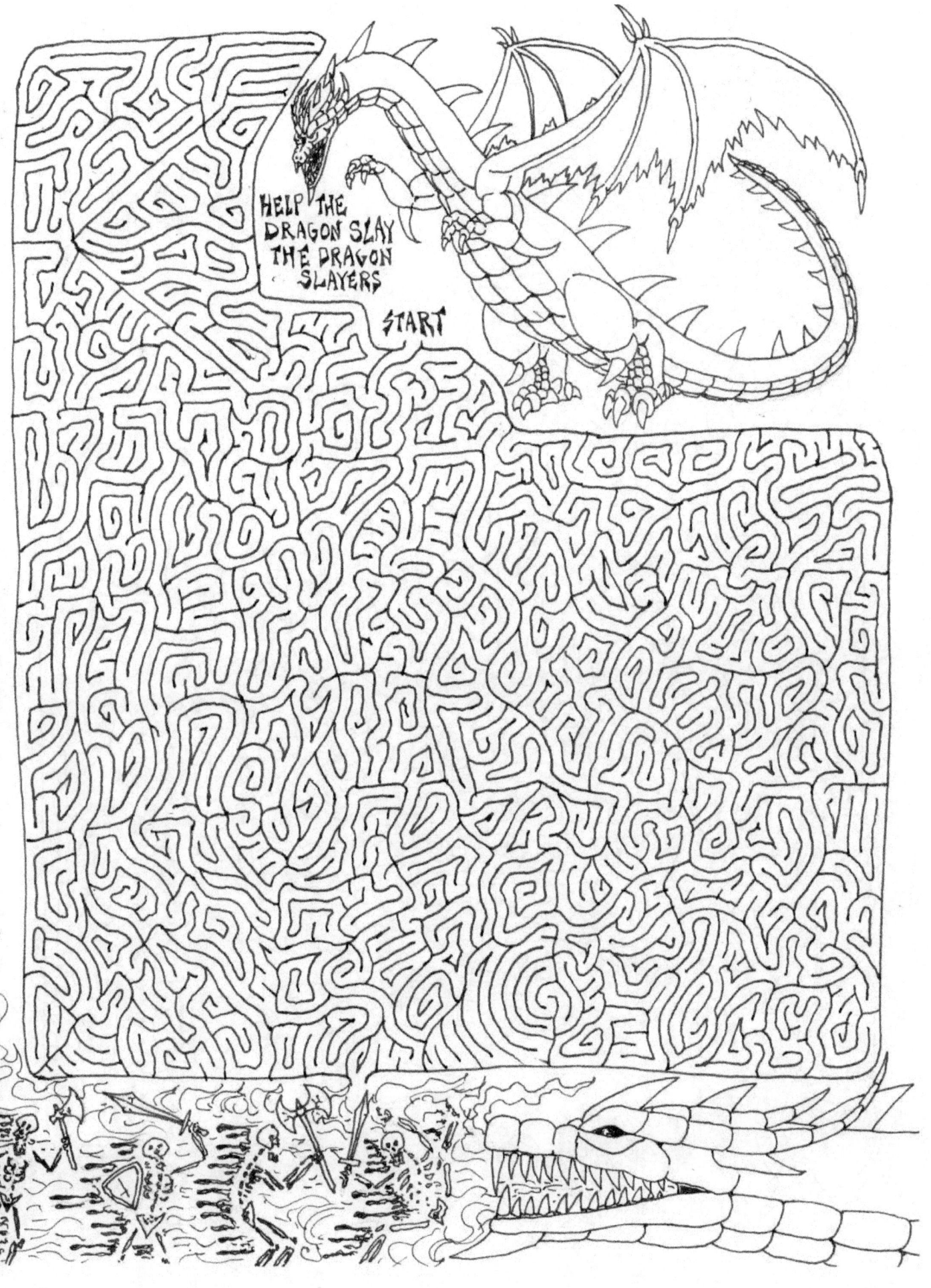

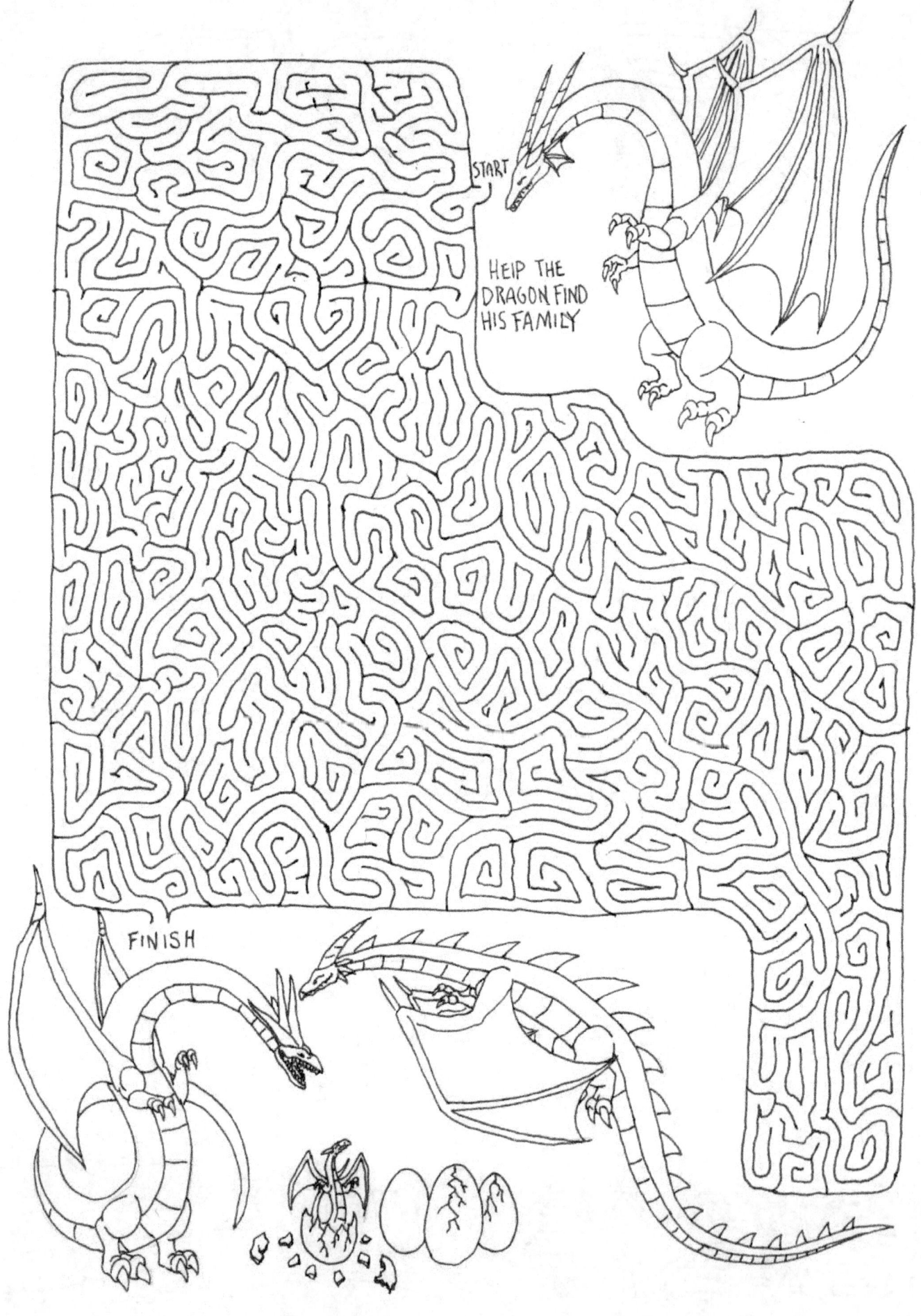

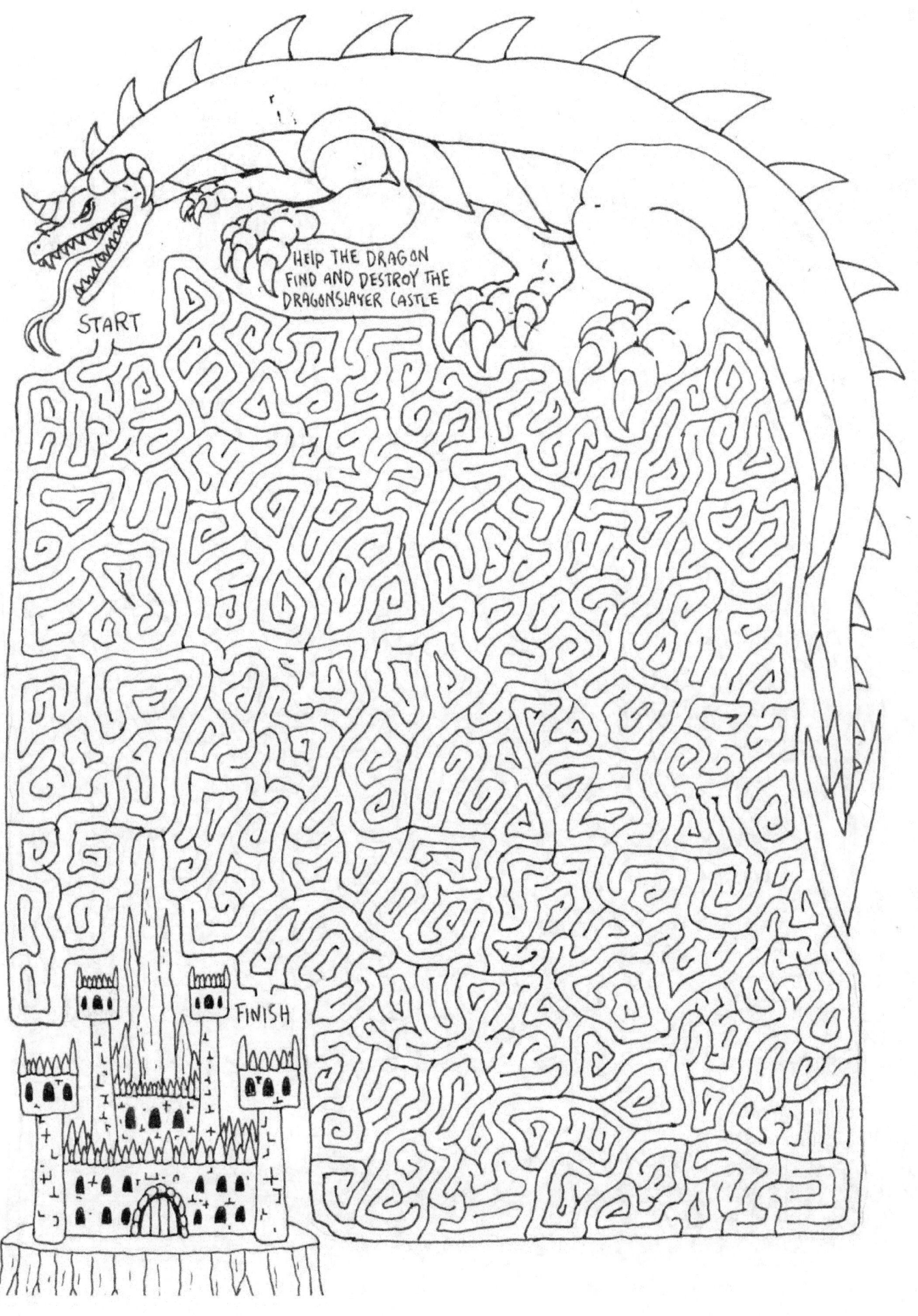

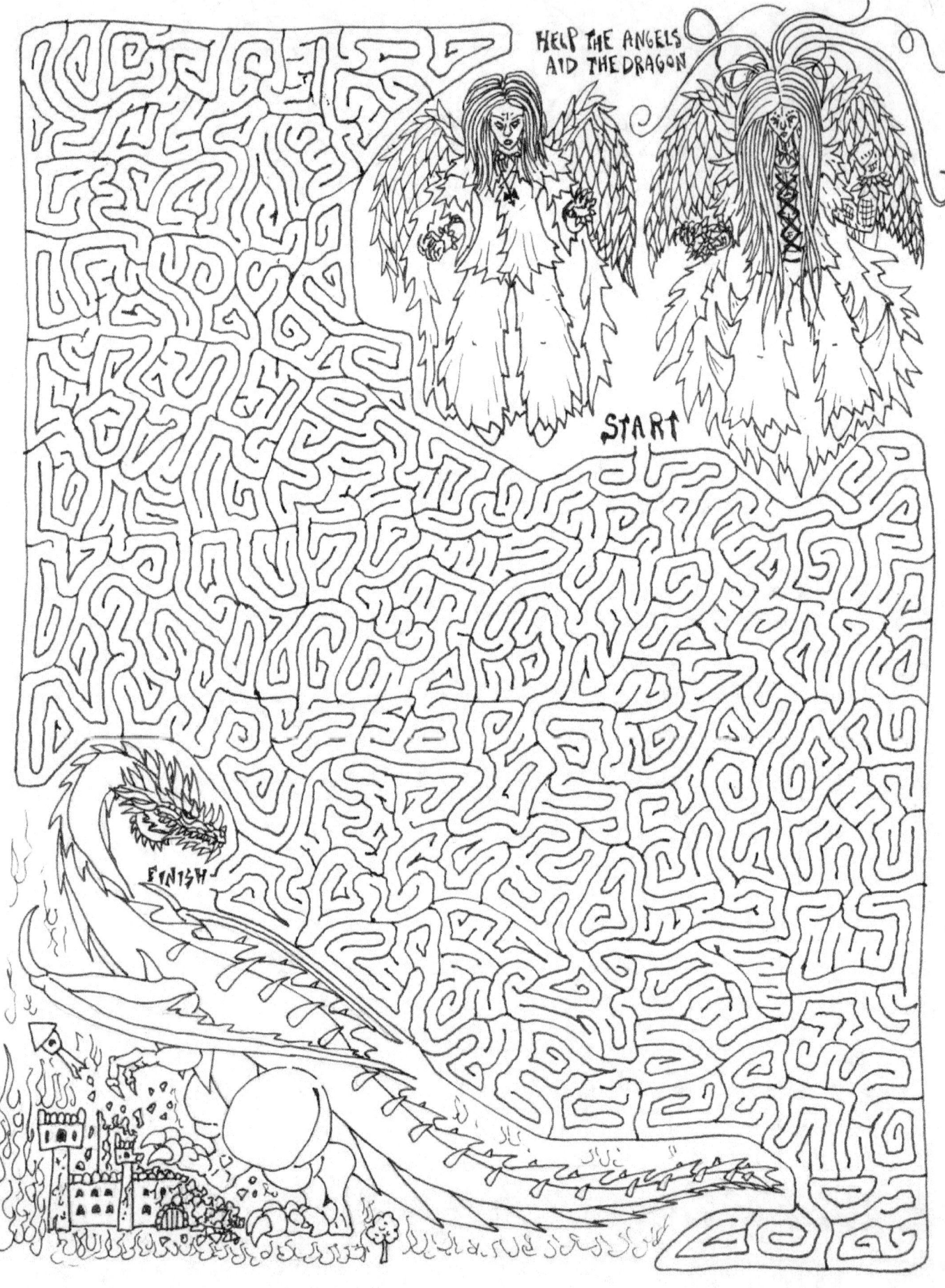

HELP THE ANGELS AID THE DRAGON

START

FINISH

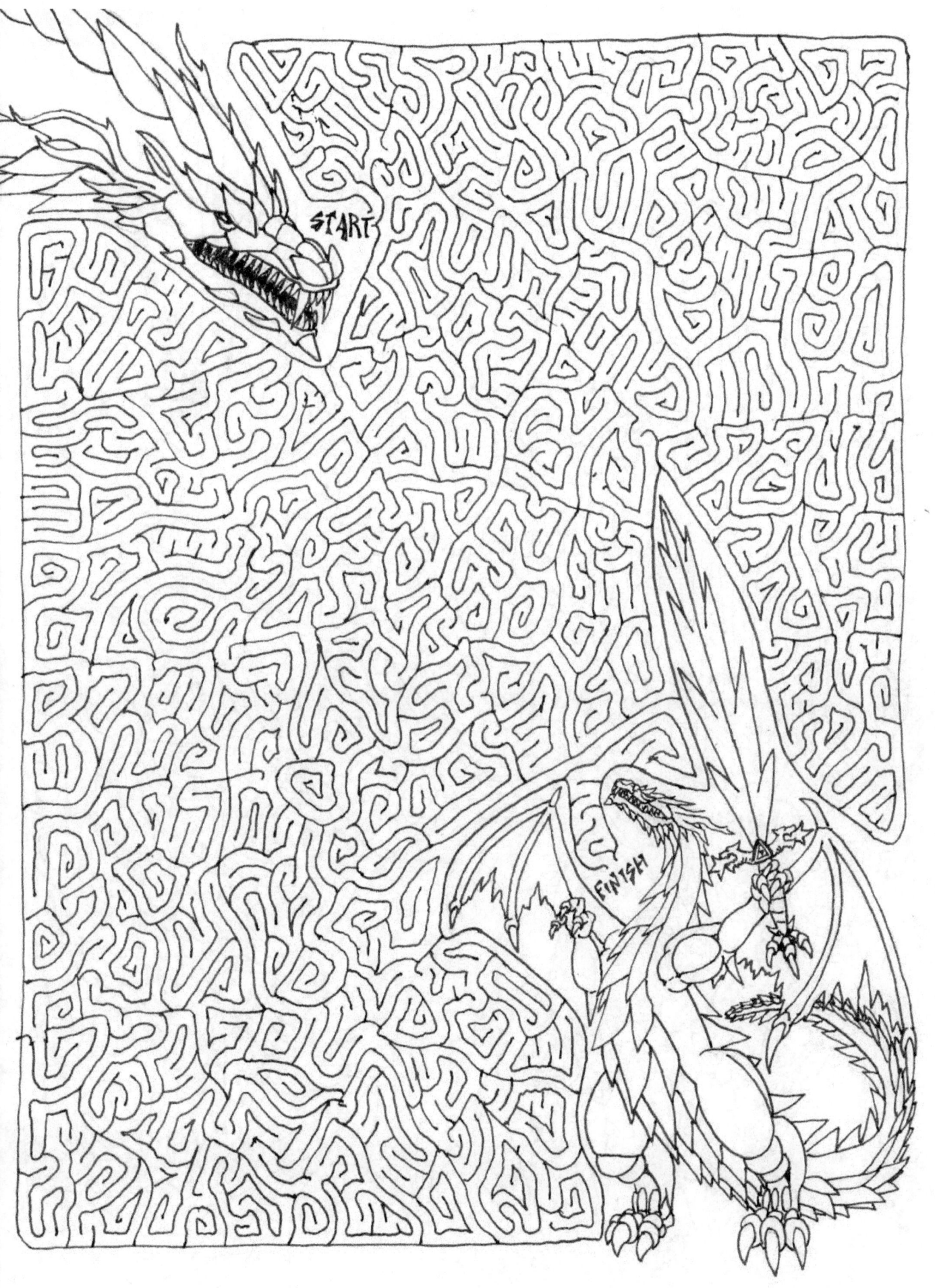

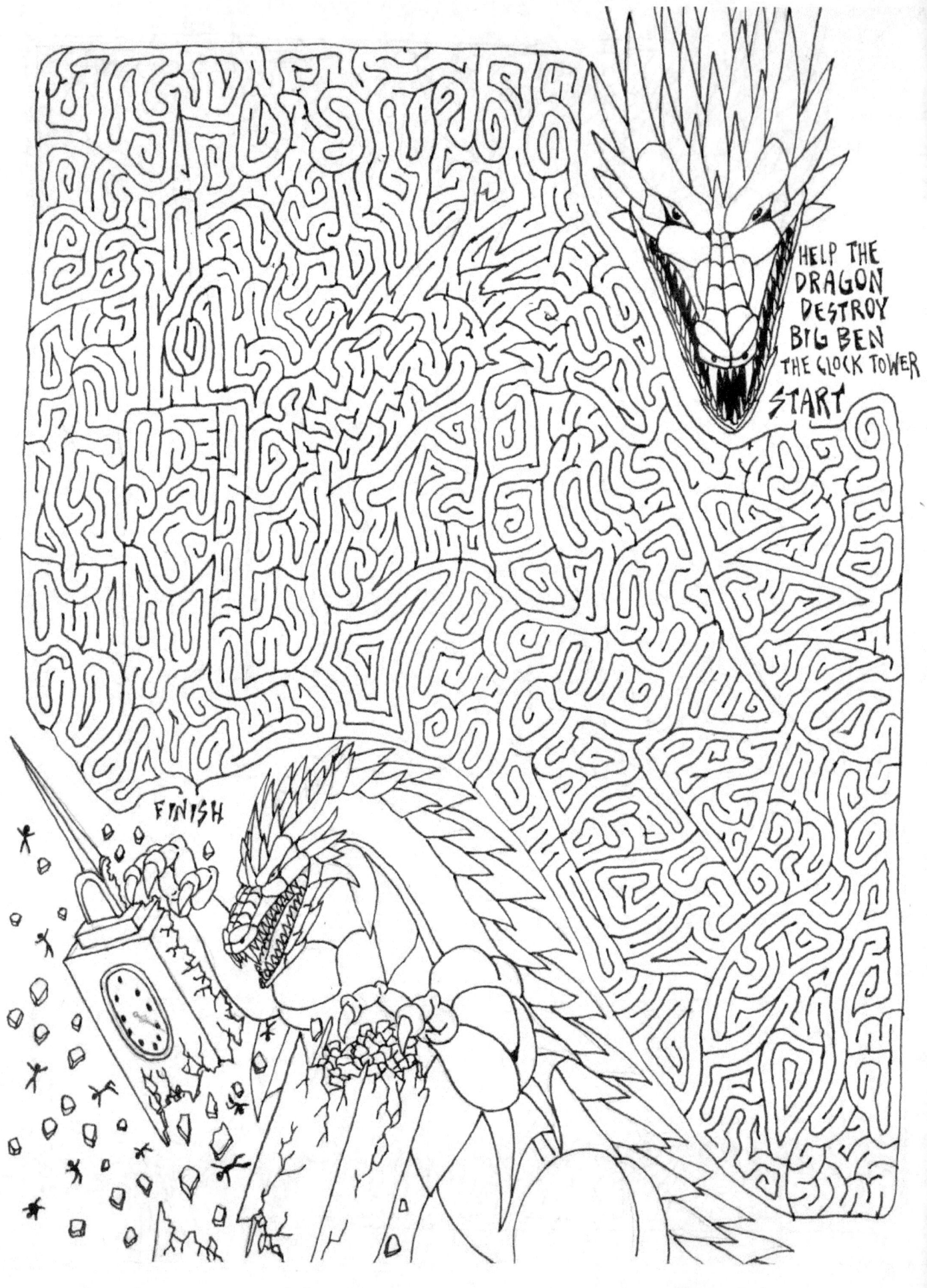

HELP THE DRAGON DESTROY BIG BEN THE CLOCK TOWER

START

FINISH

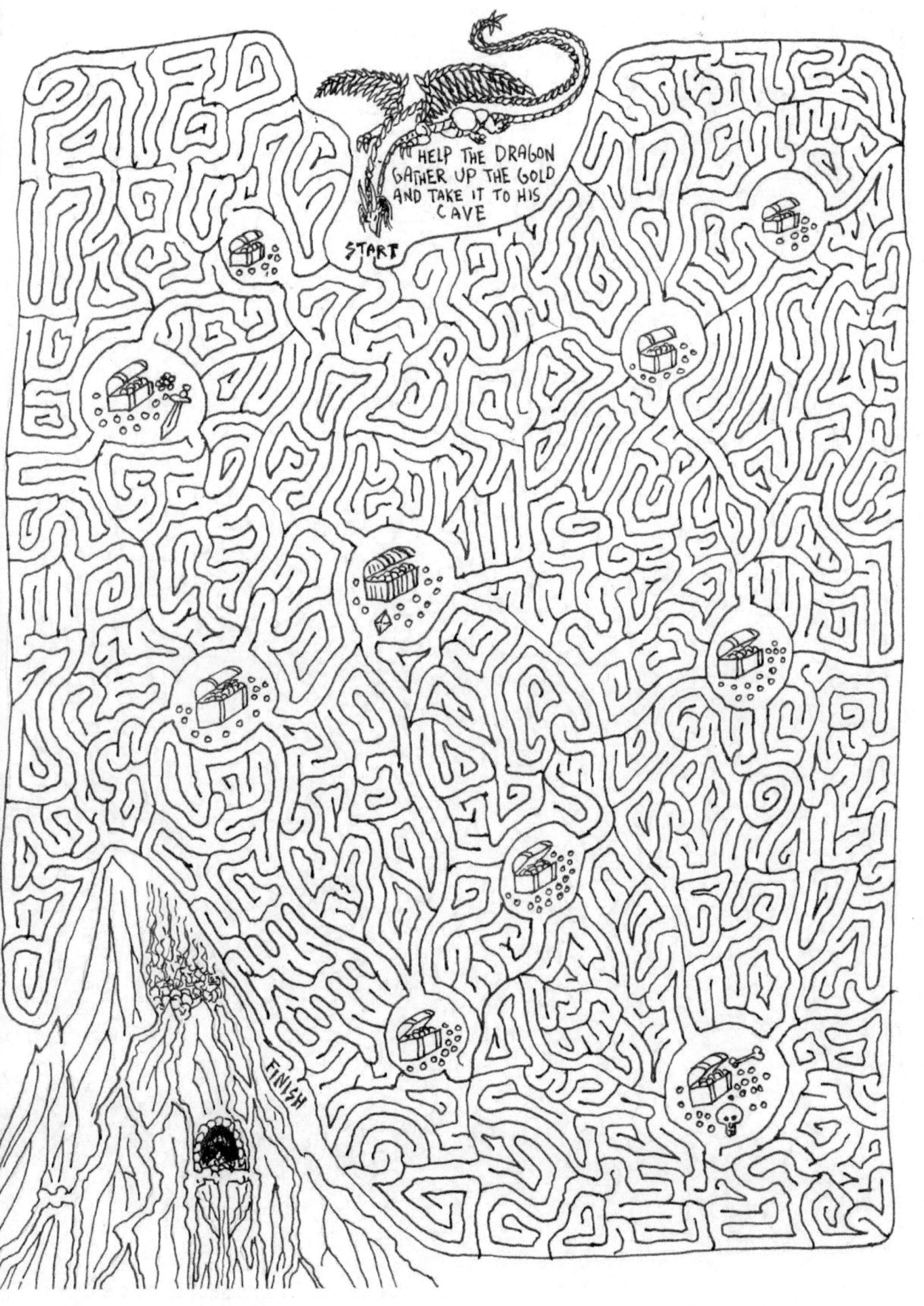

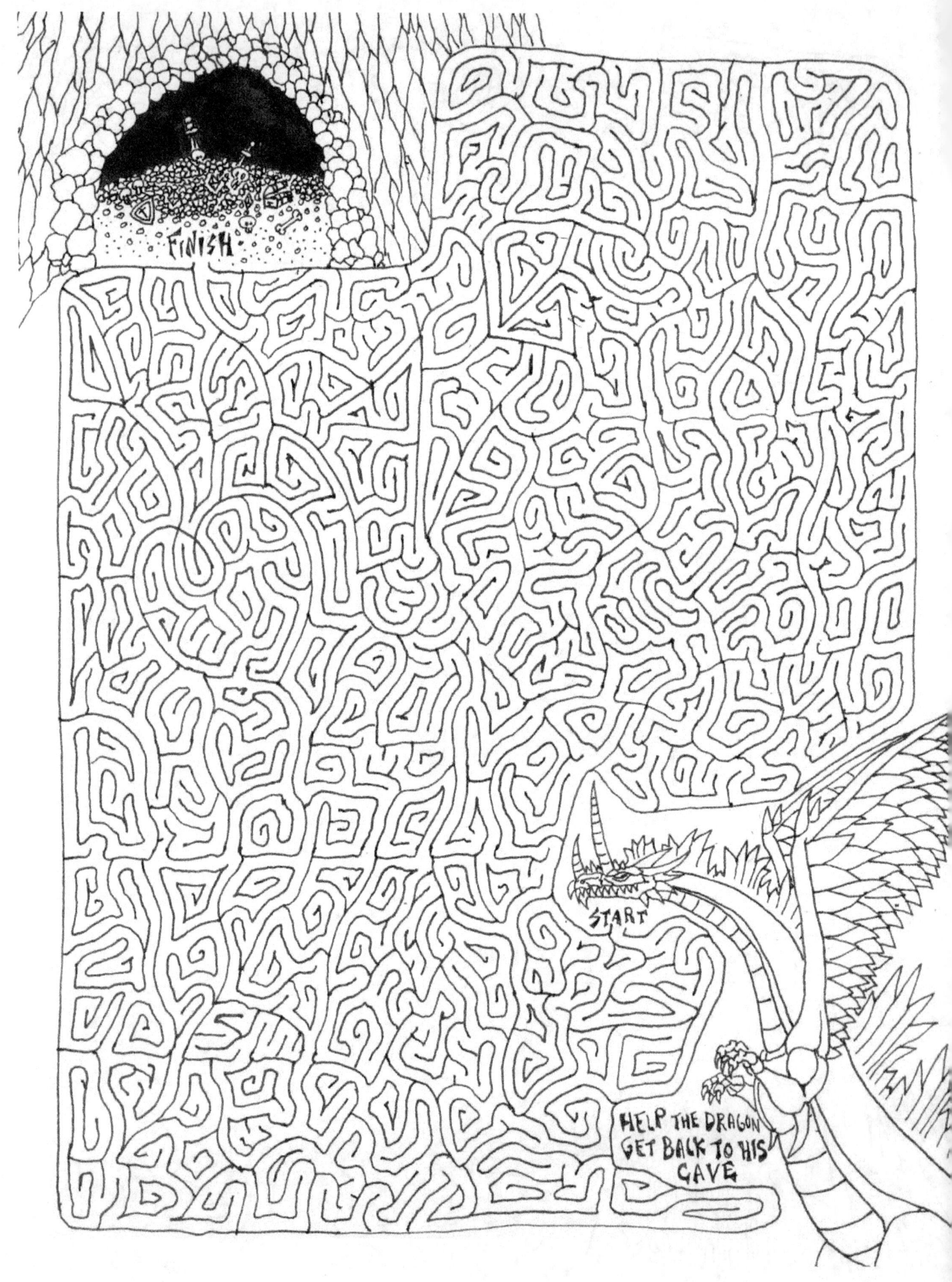

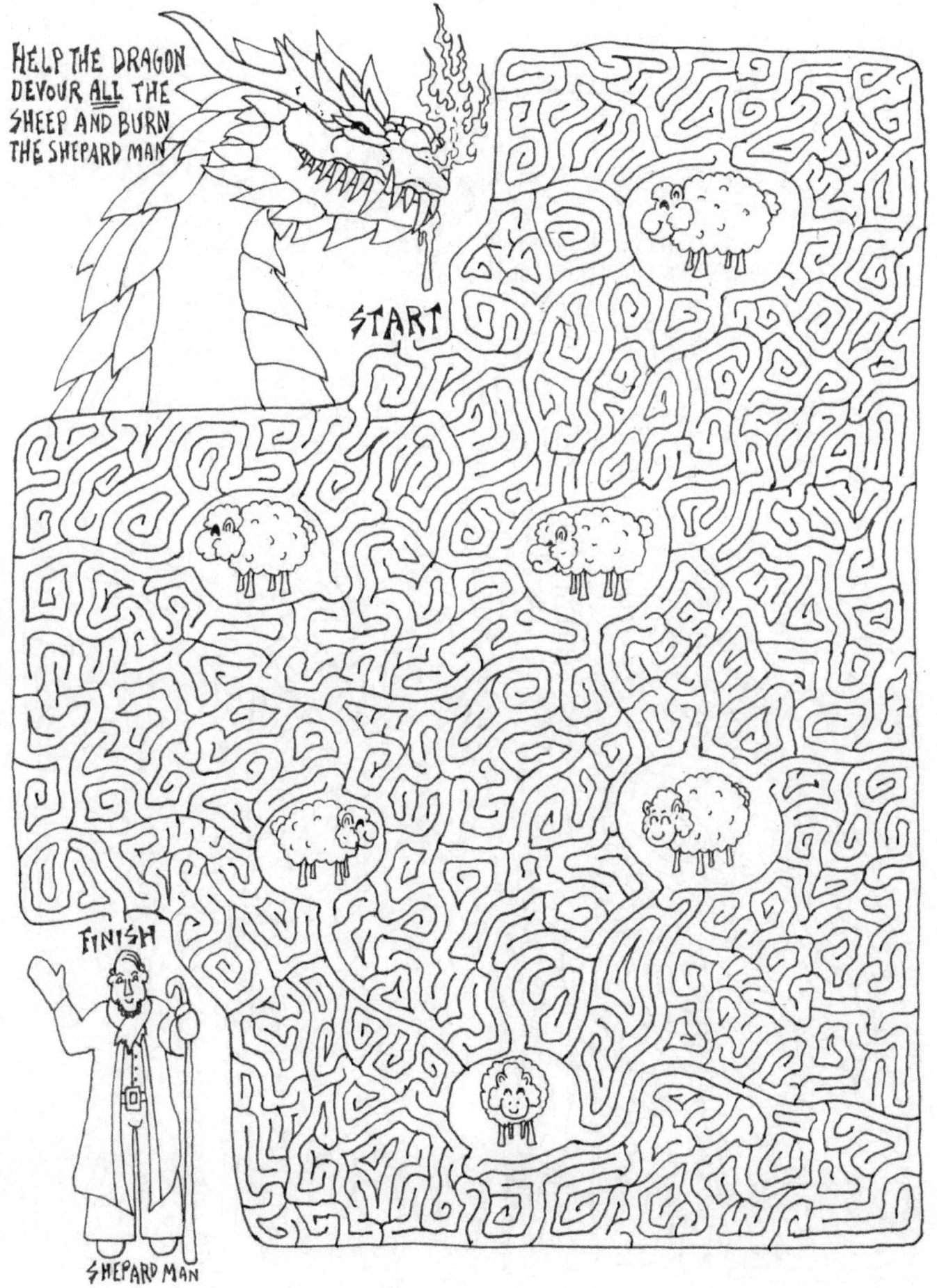

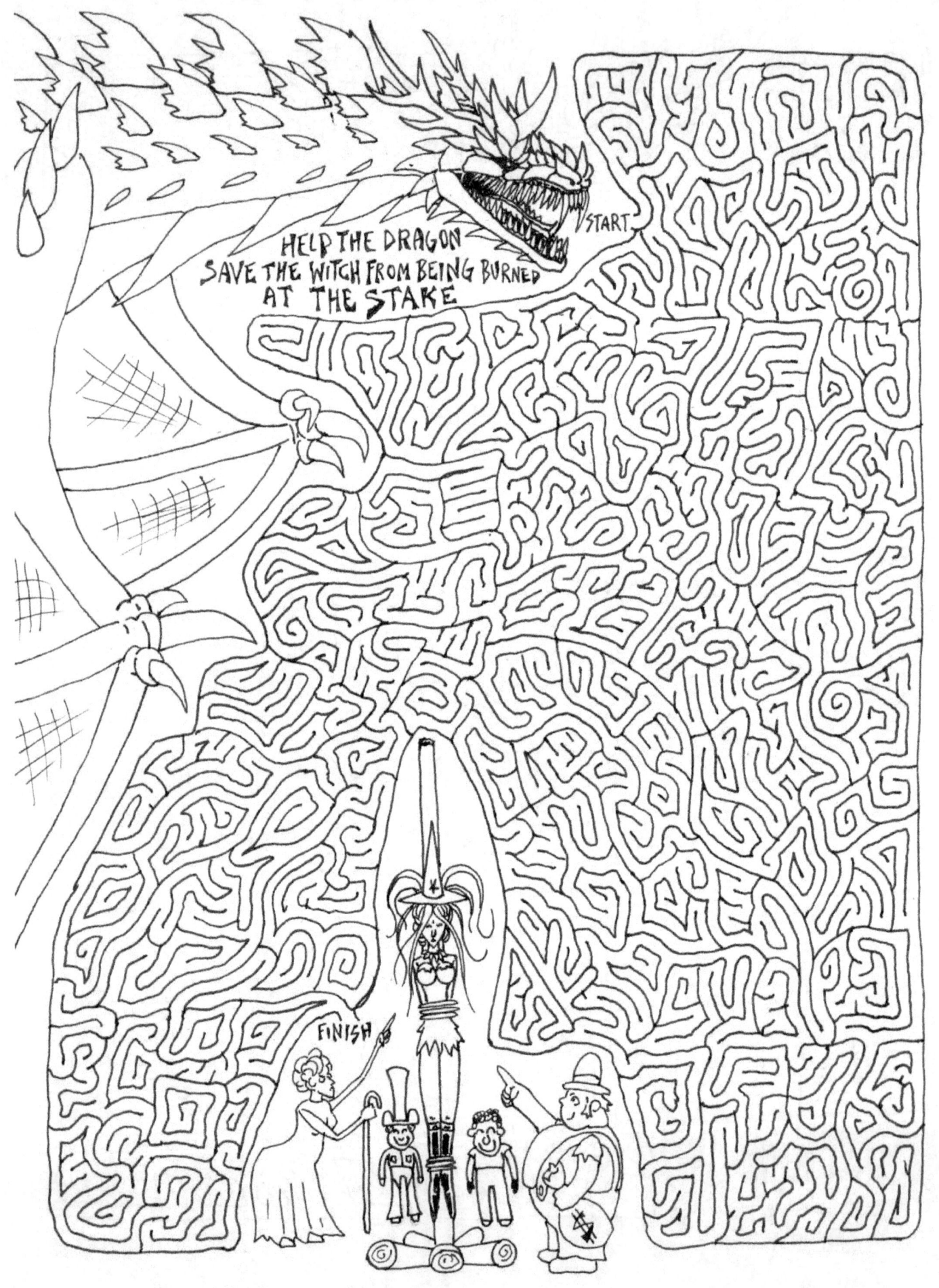

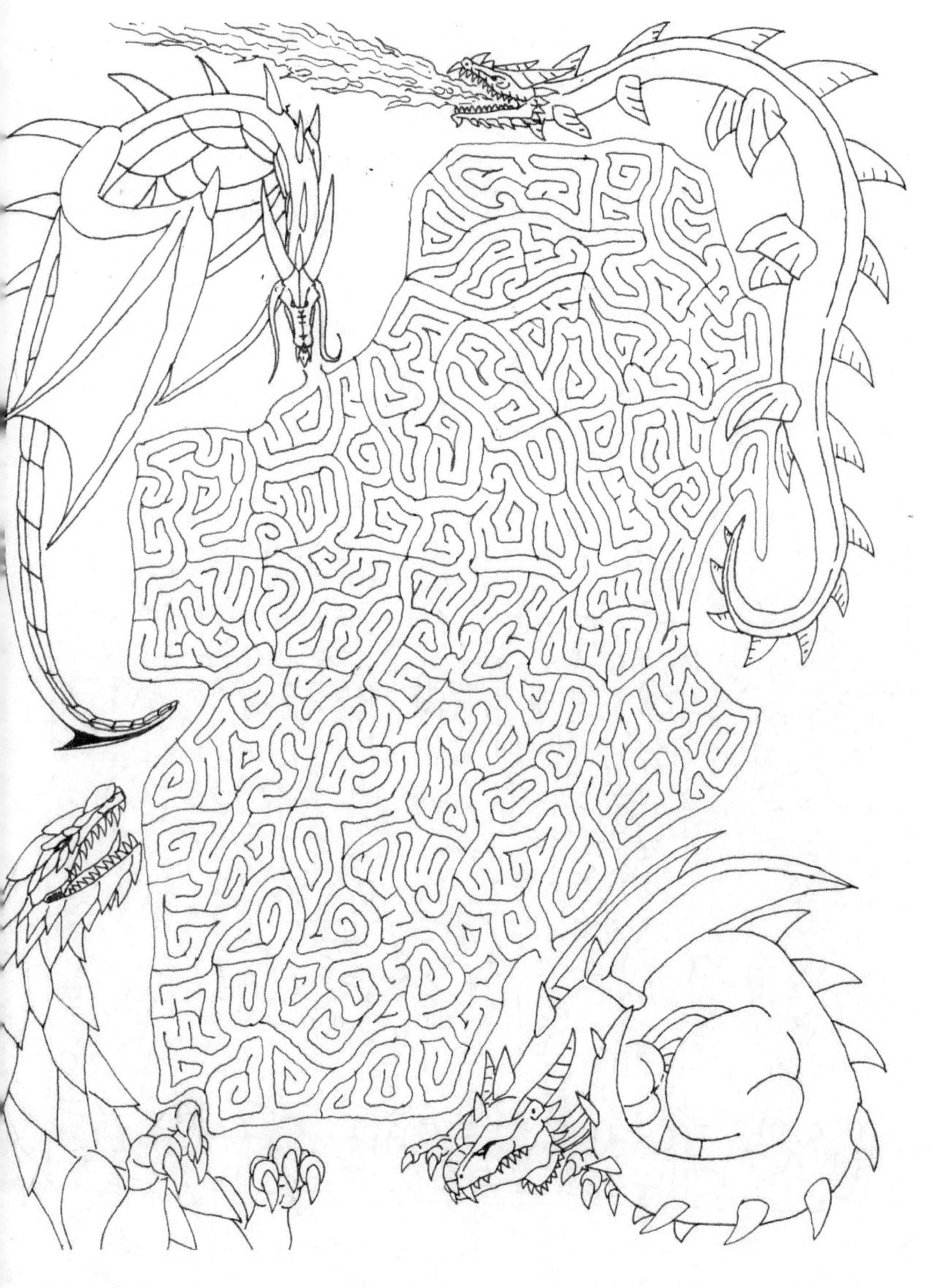

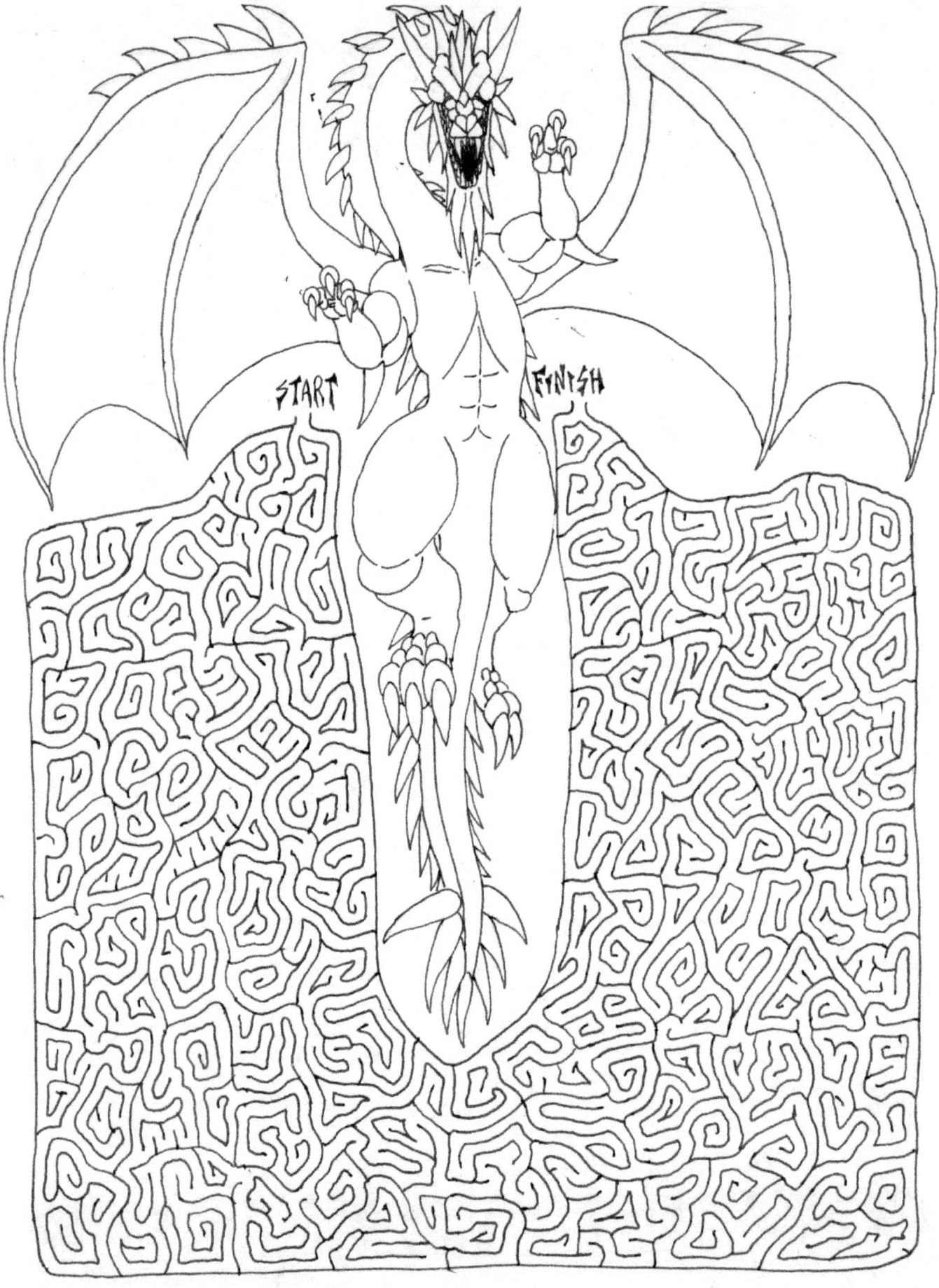

START

FINISH

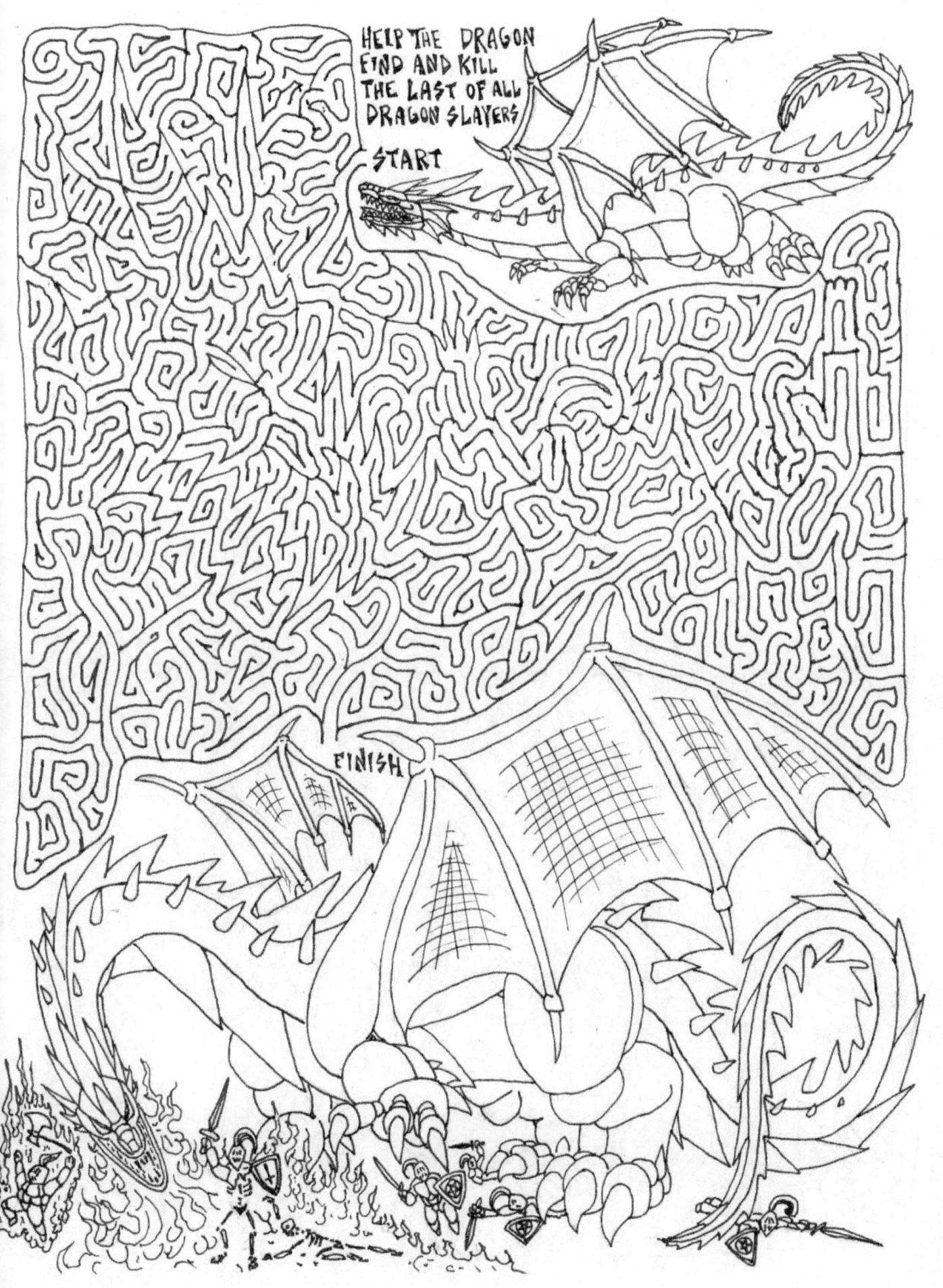

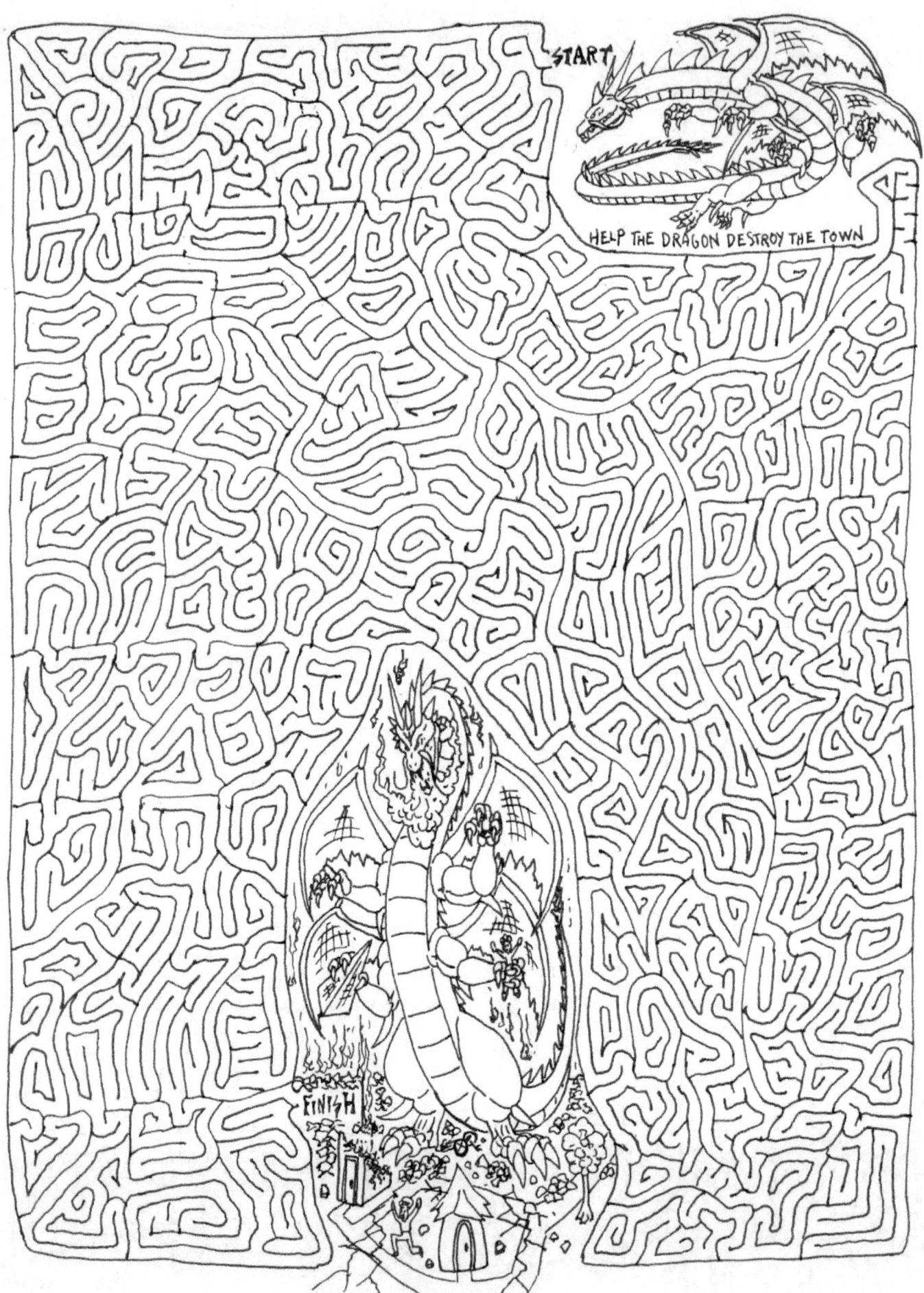

START

HELP THE DRAGON DESTROY THE TOWN

FINISH

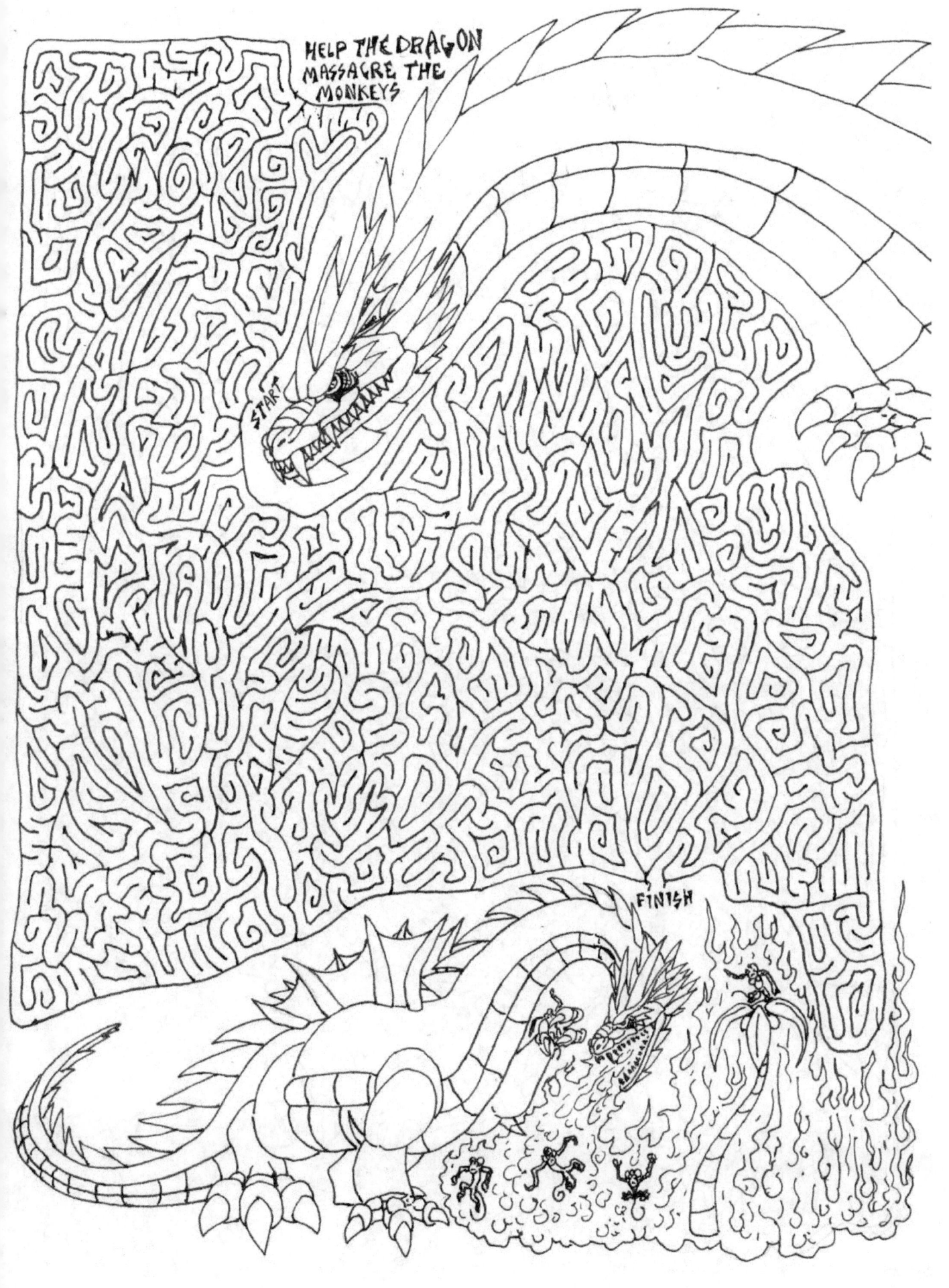

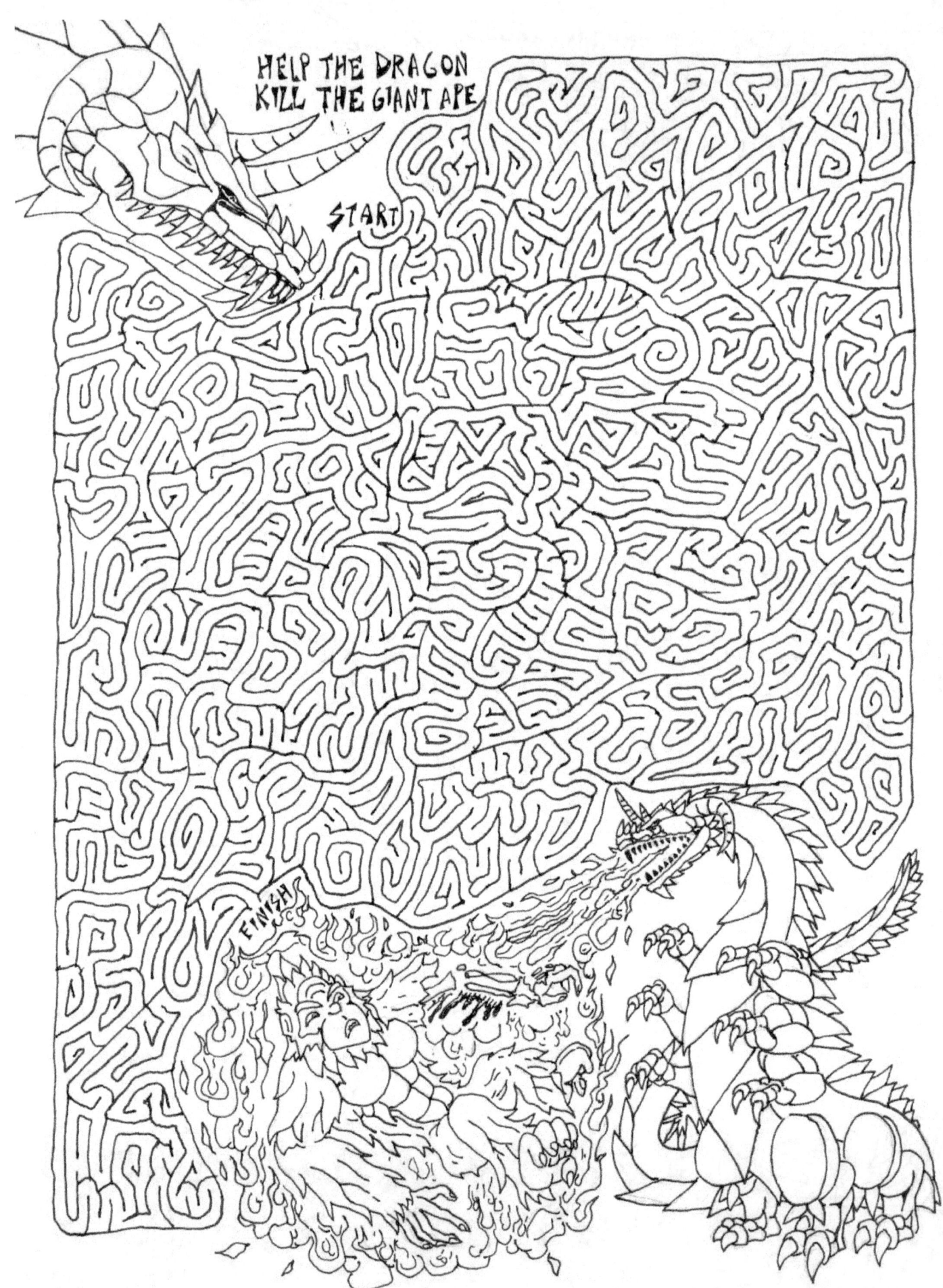

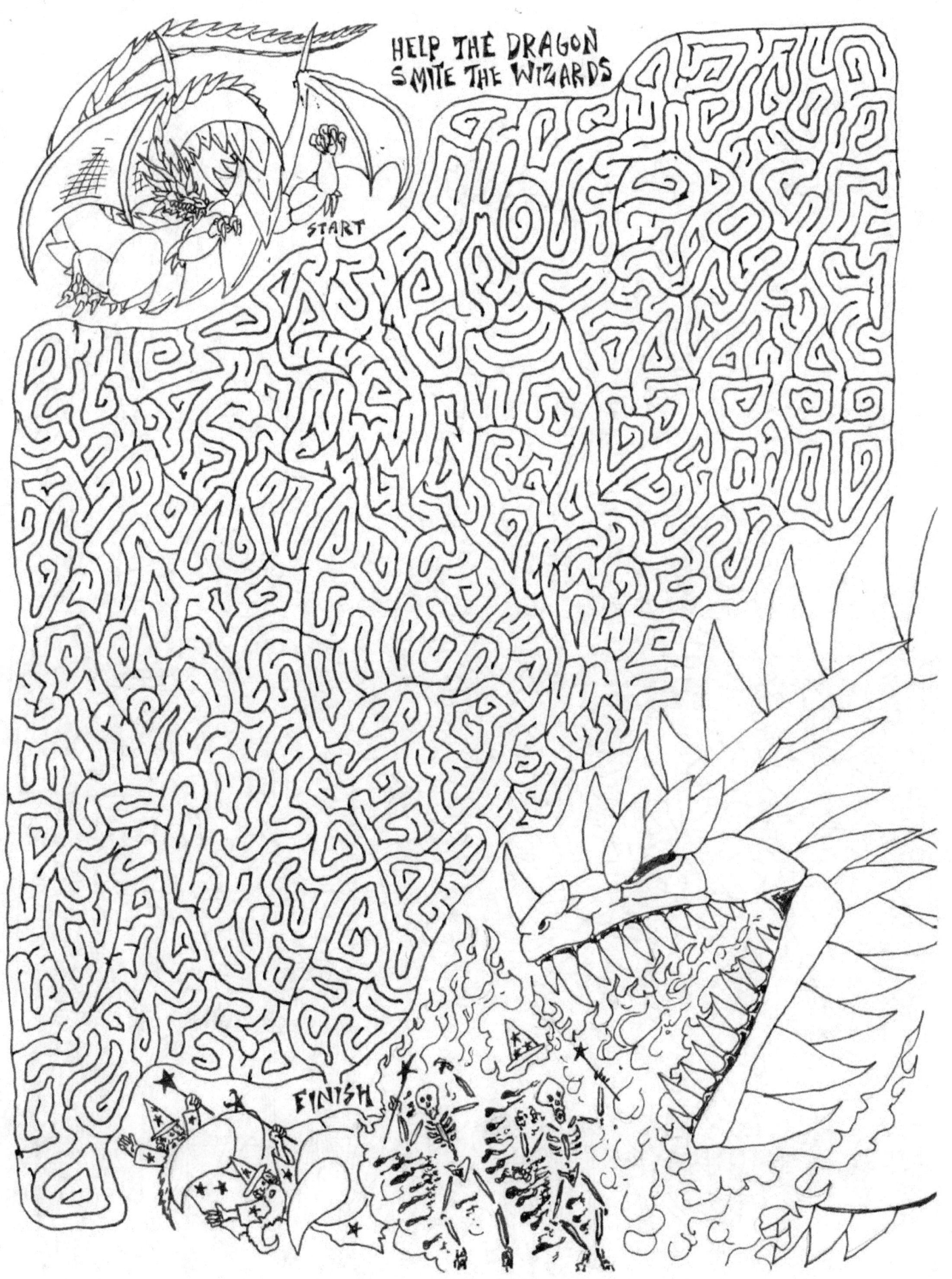

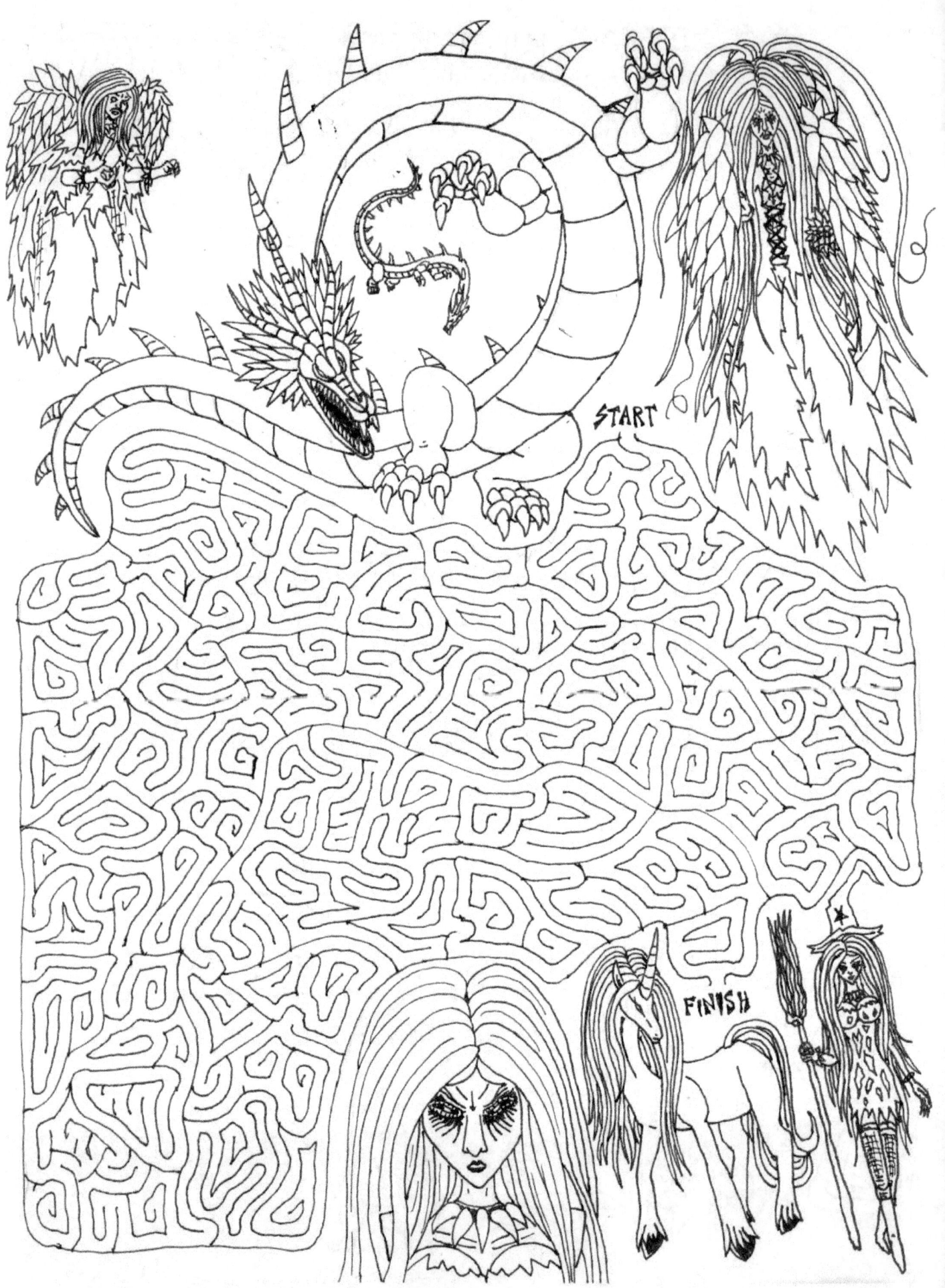

START

FINISH

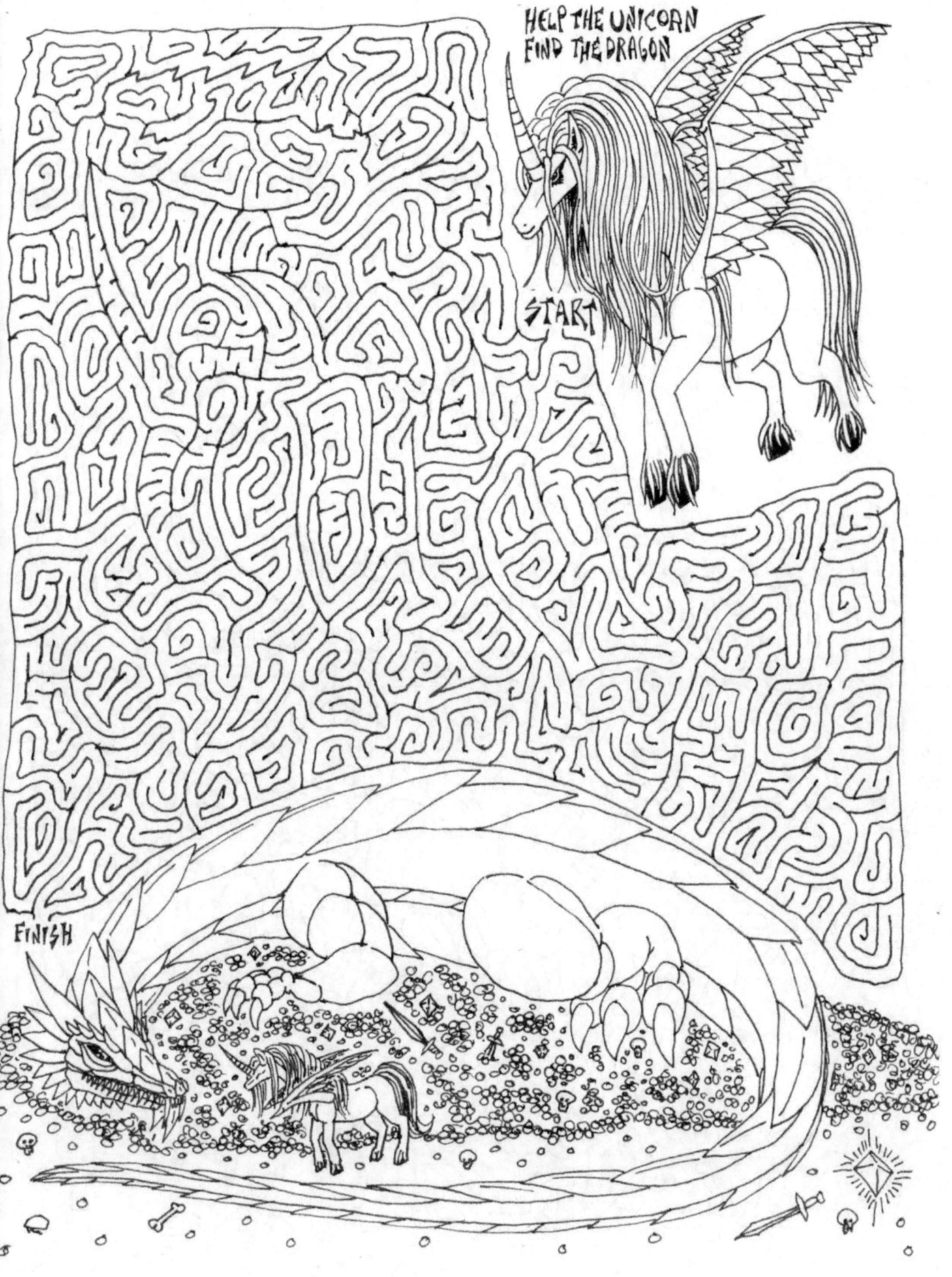

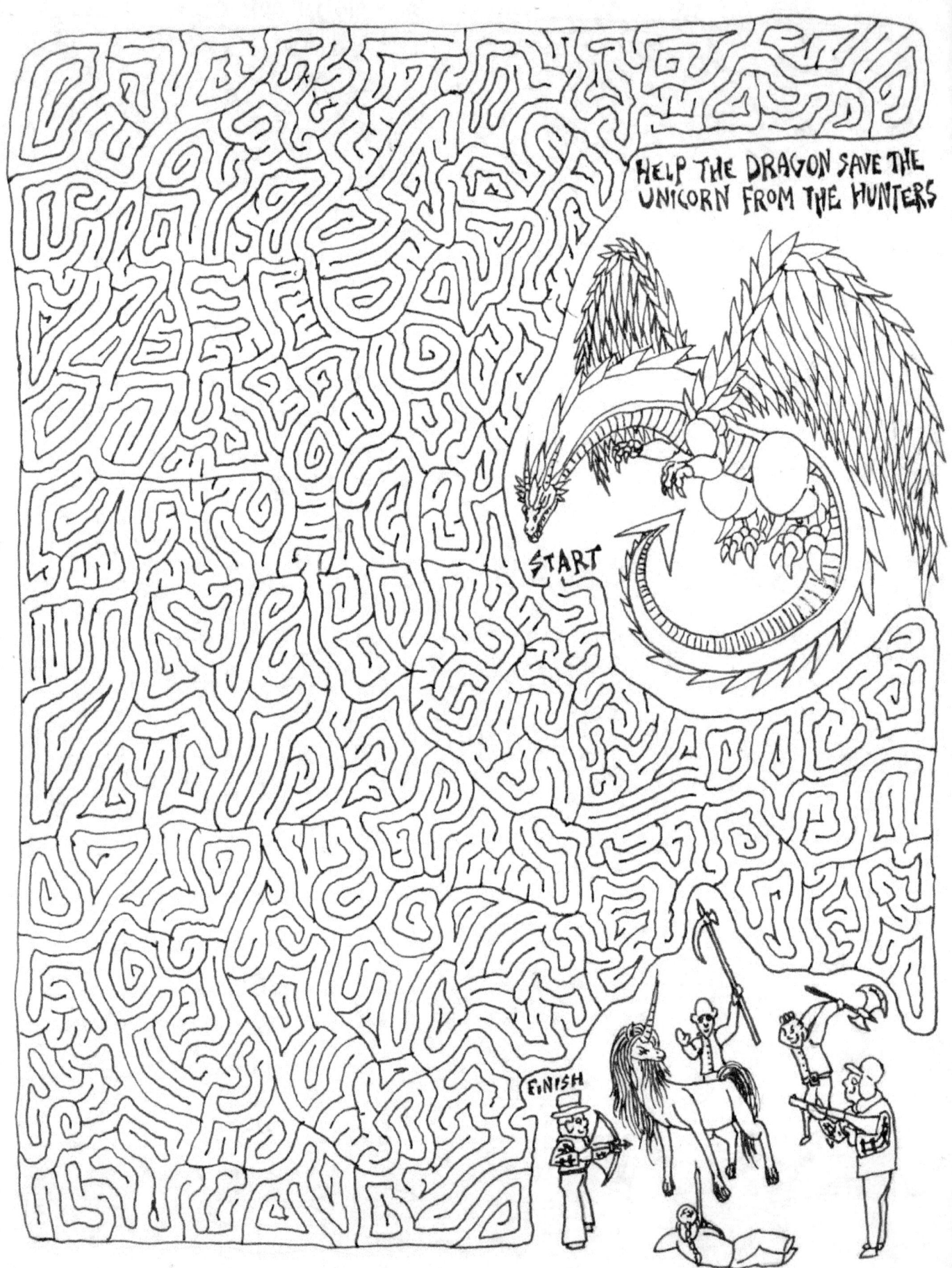

HELP THE DRAGON SAVE THE
UNICORN FROM THE HUNTERS

START

FINISH

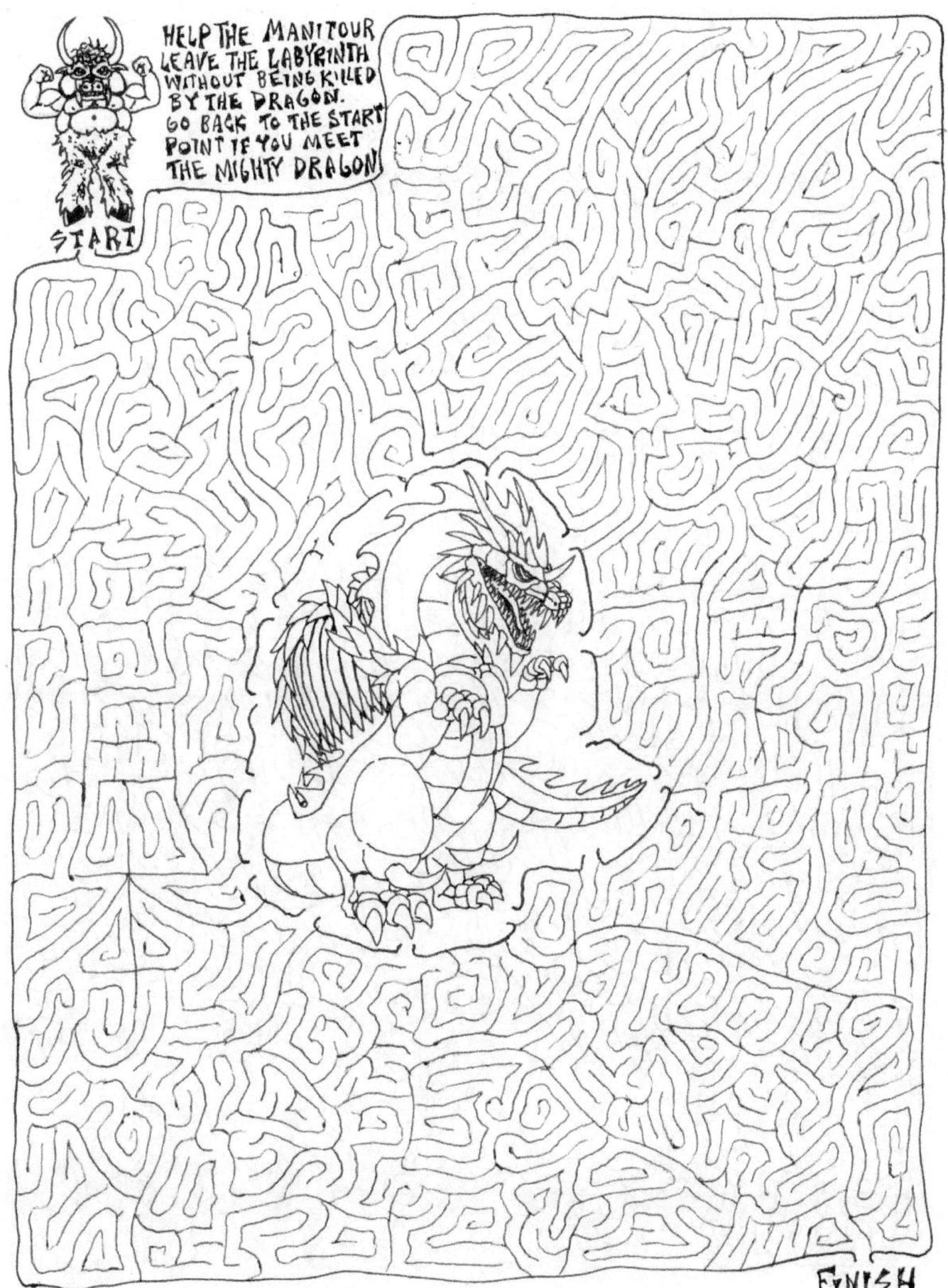

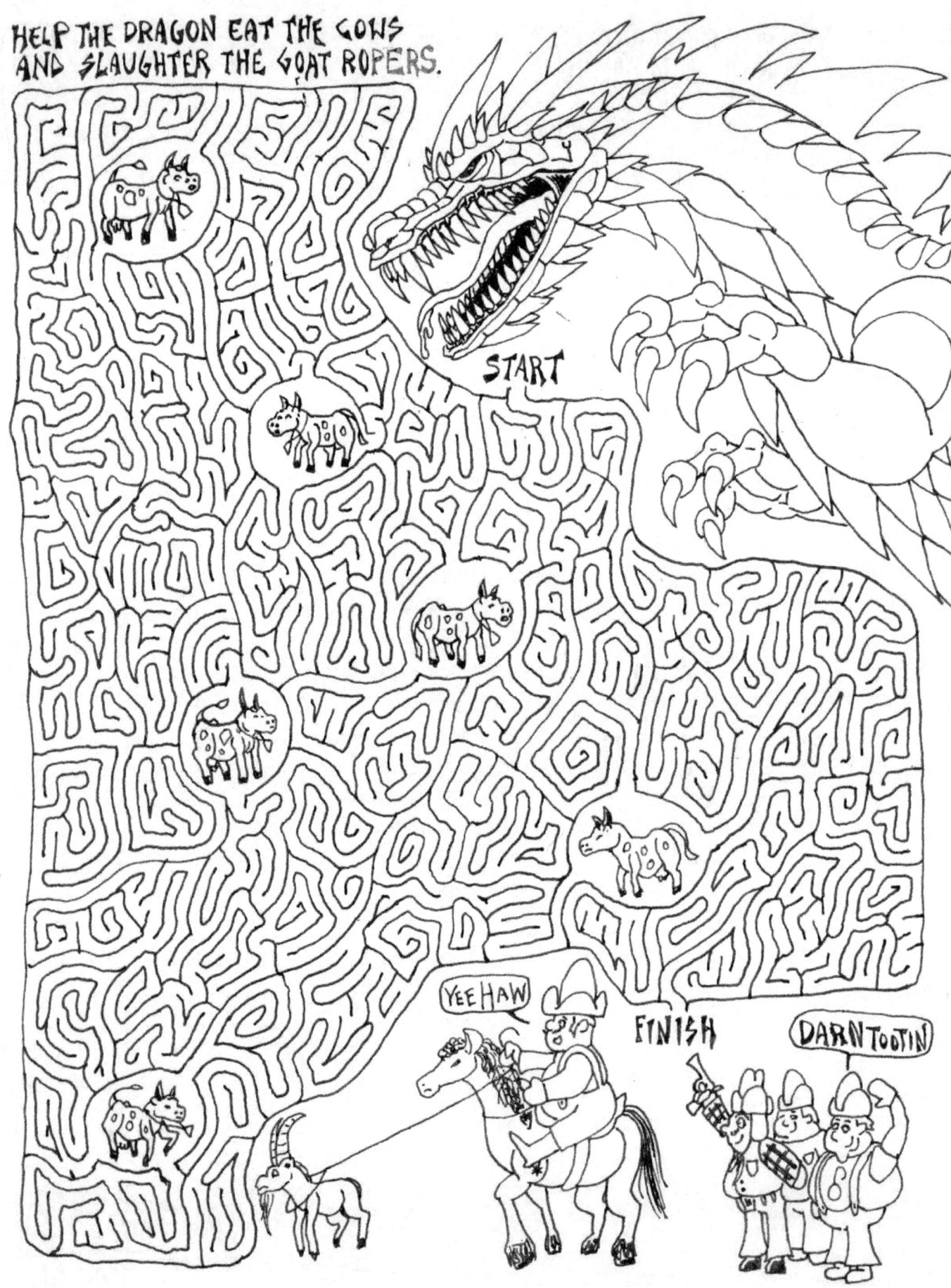

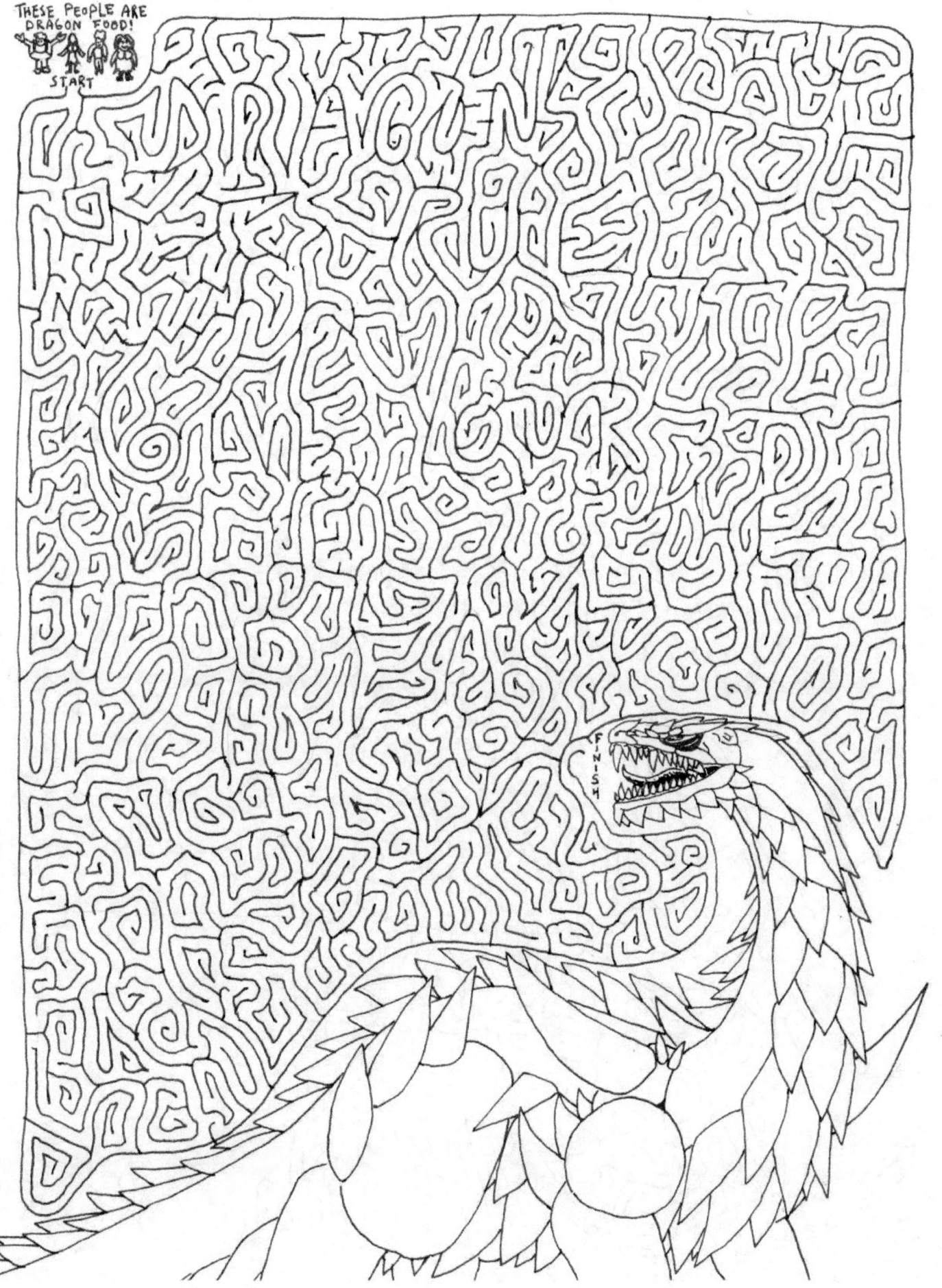

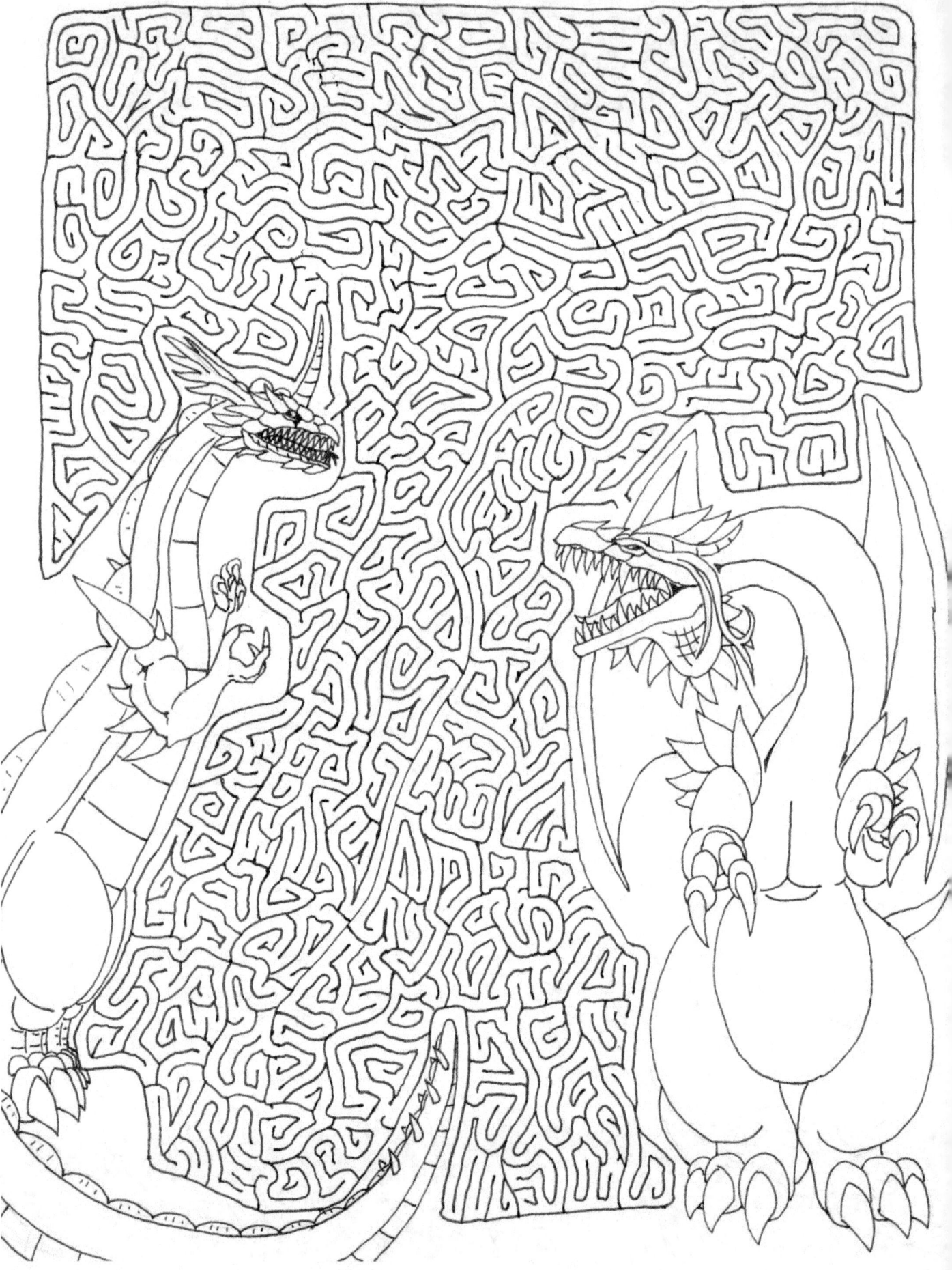

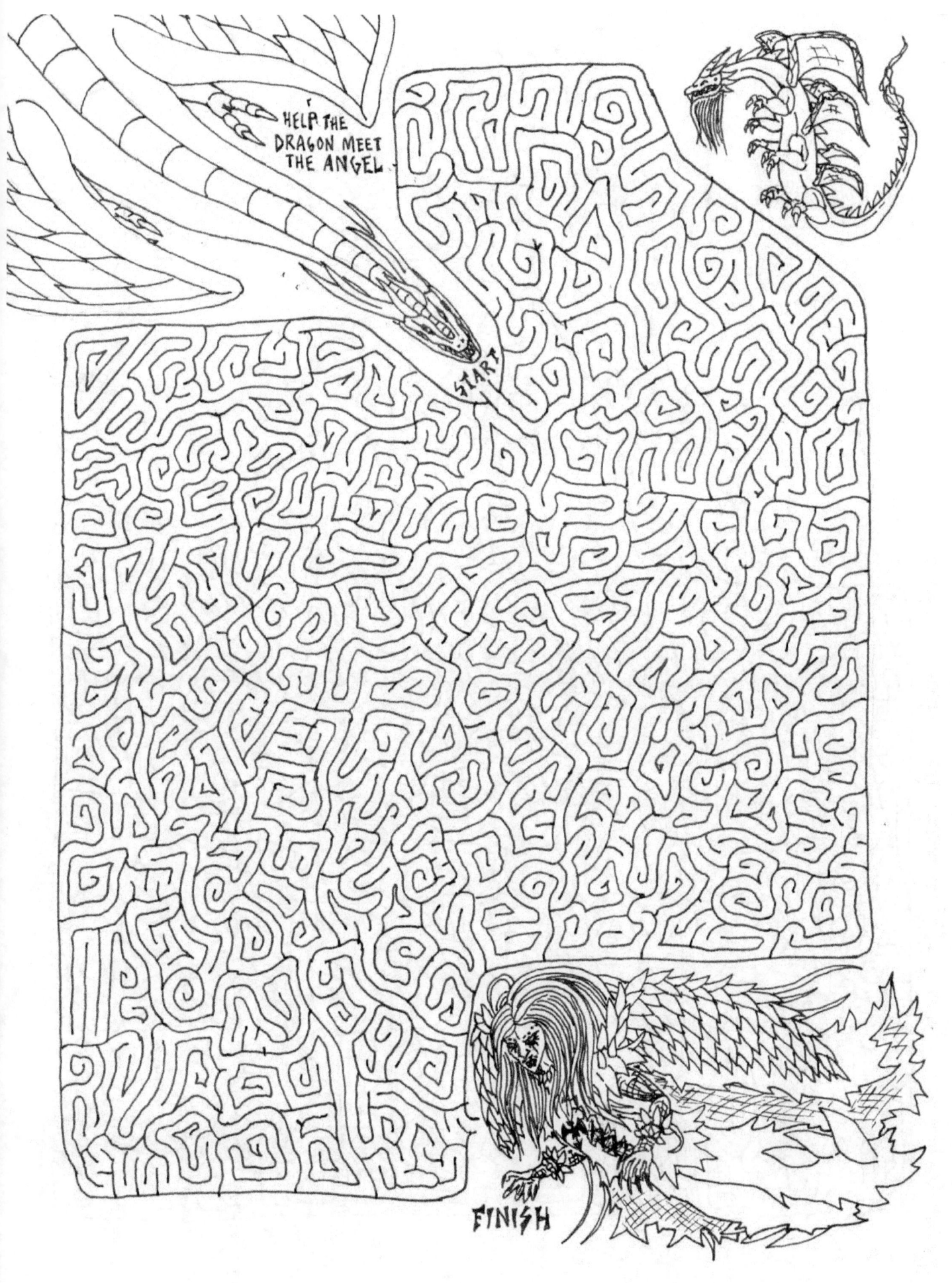

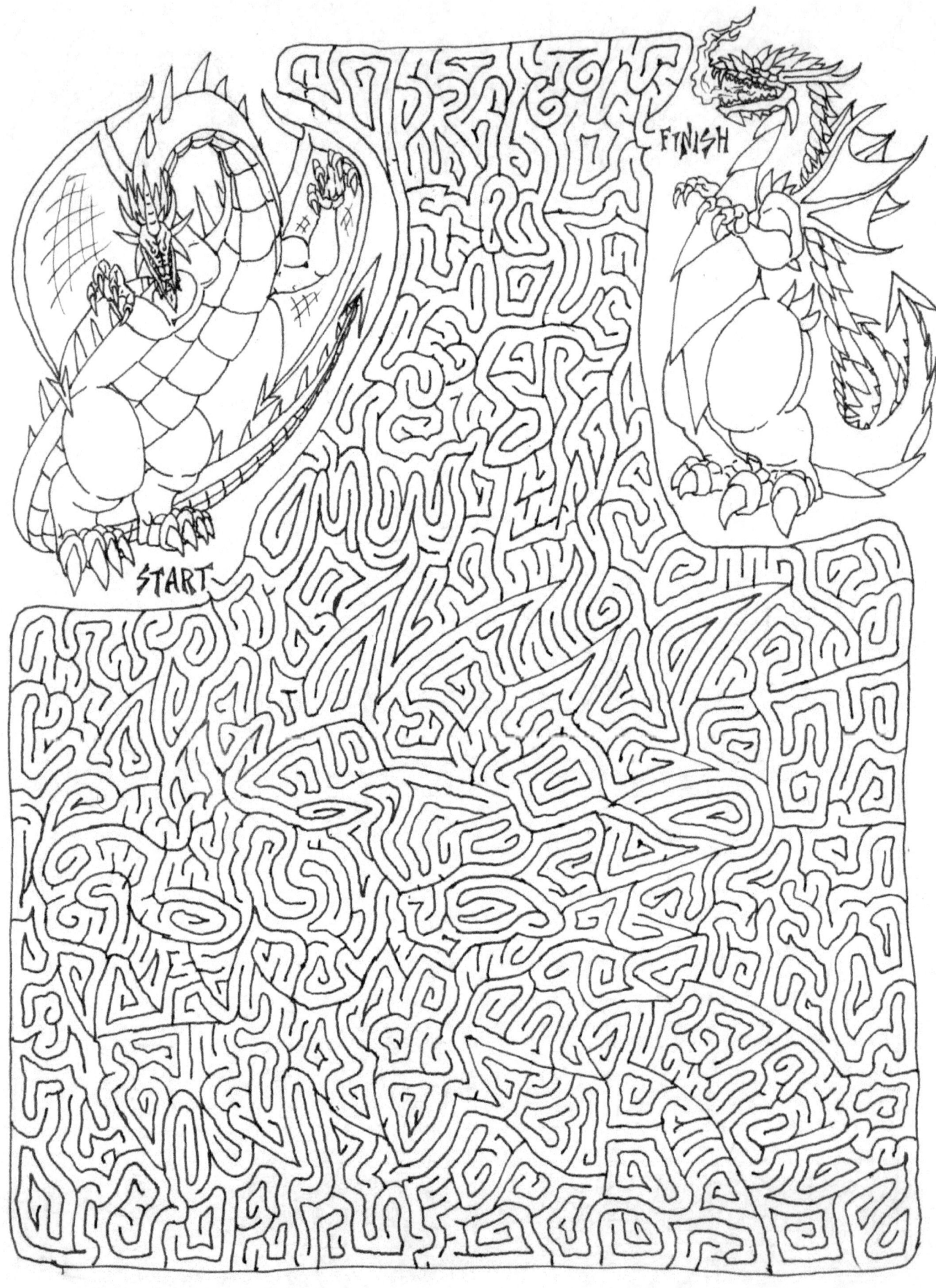

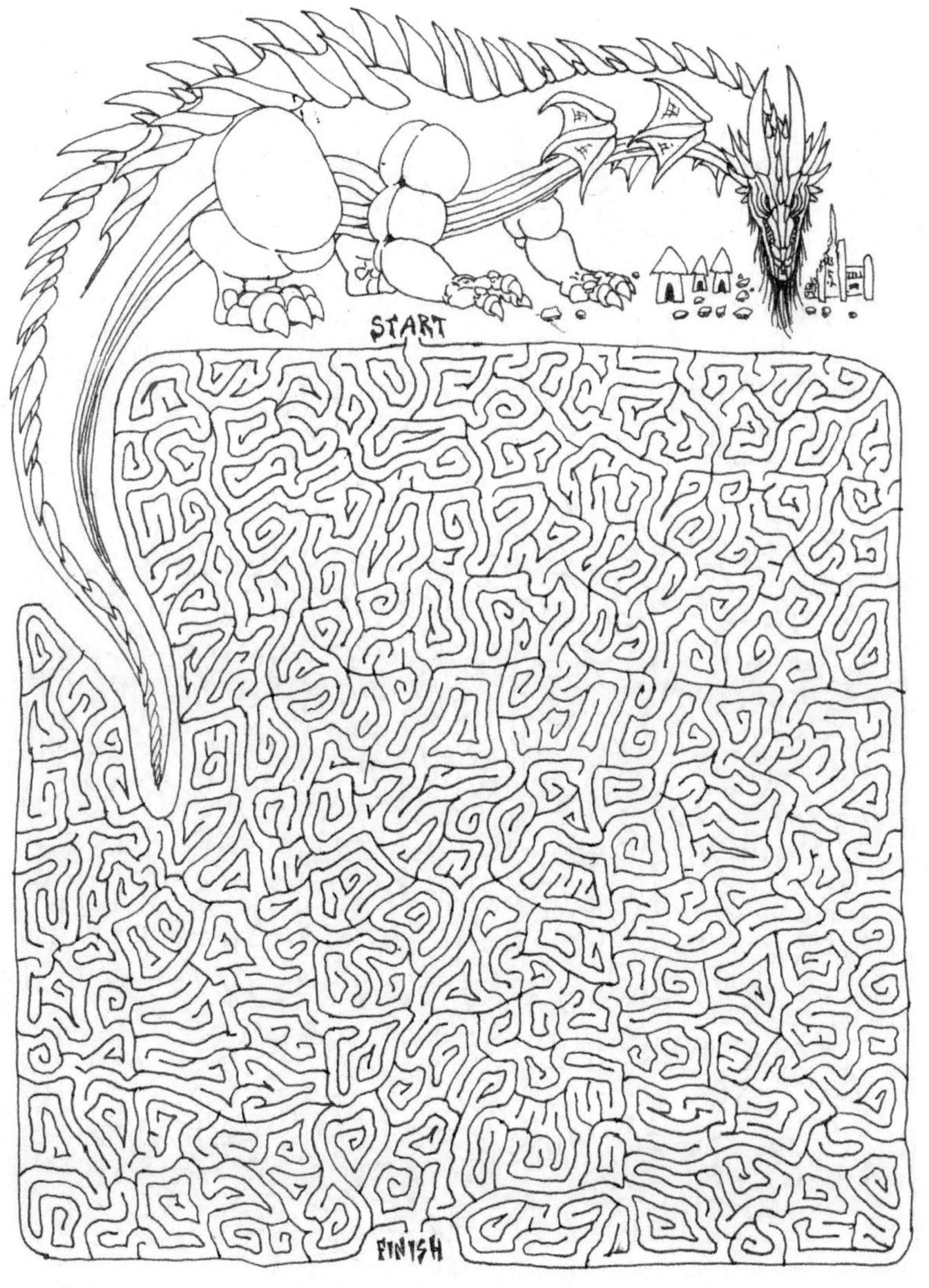

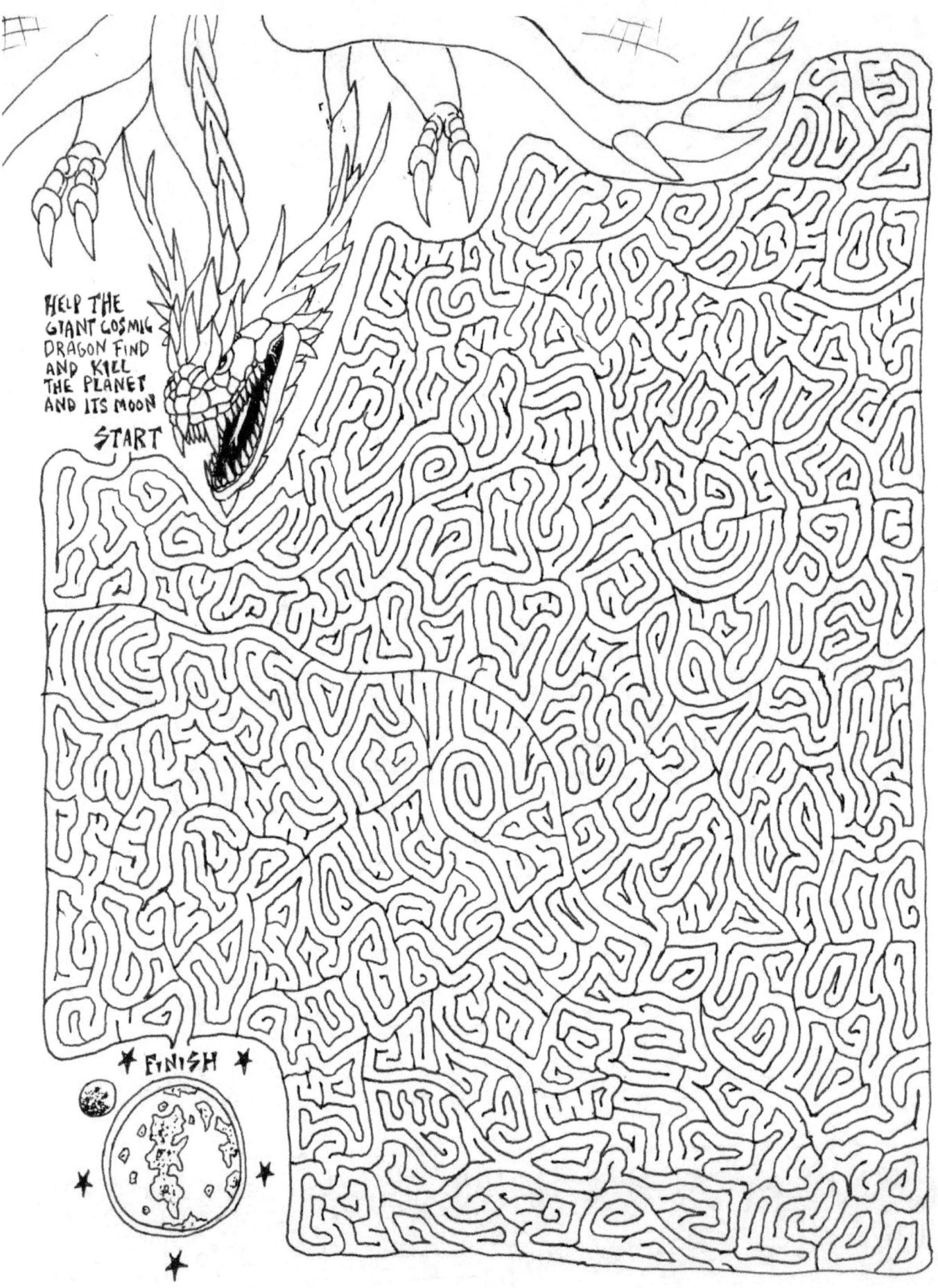

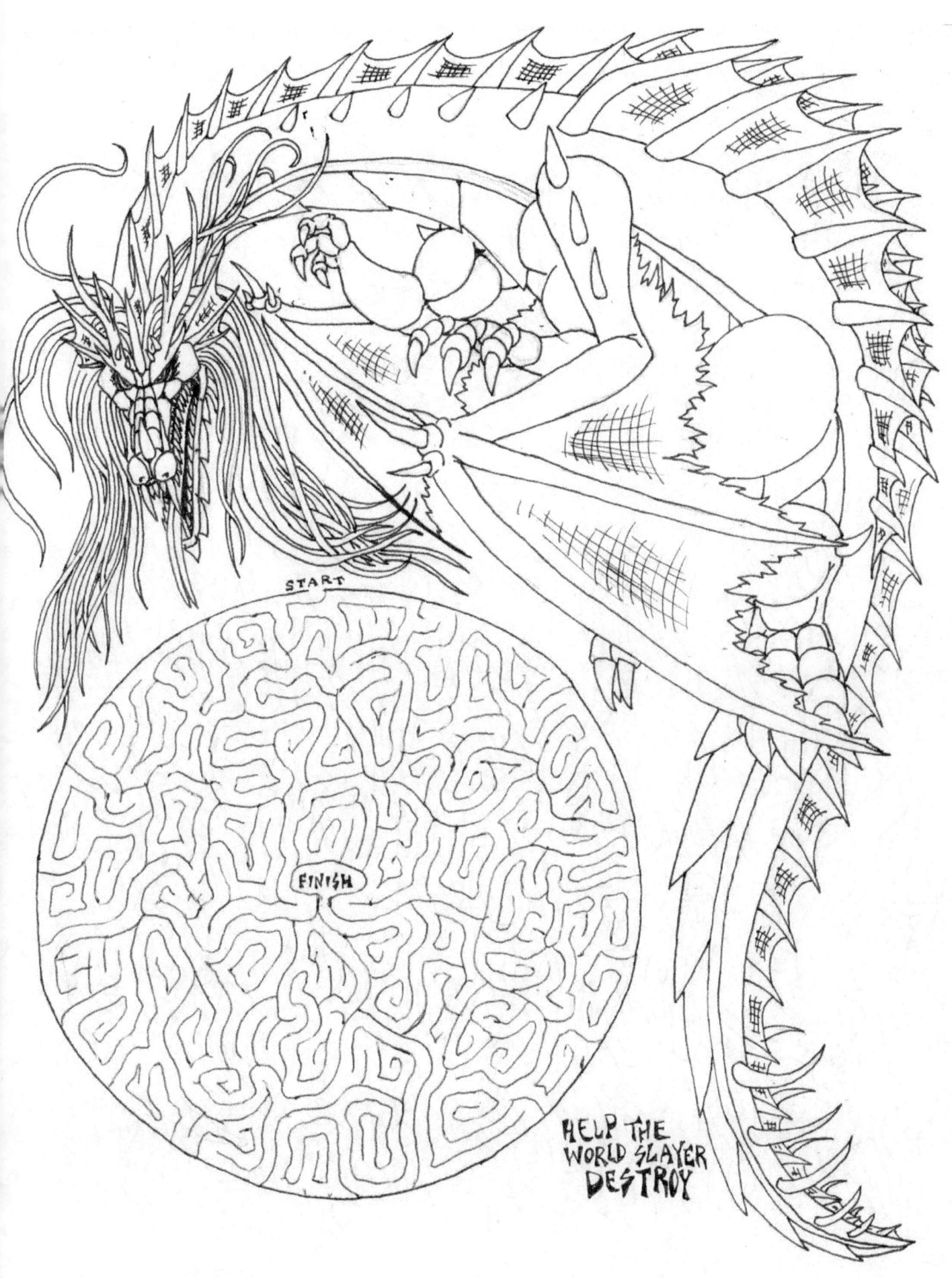

START

FINISH

HELP THE
WORLD SLAYER
DESTROY

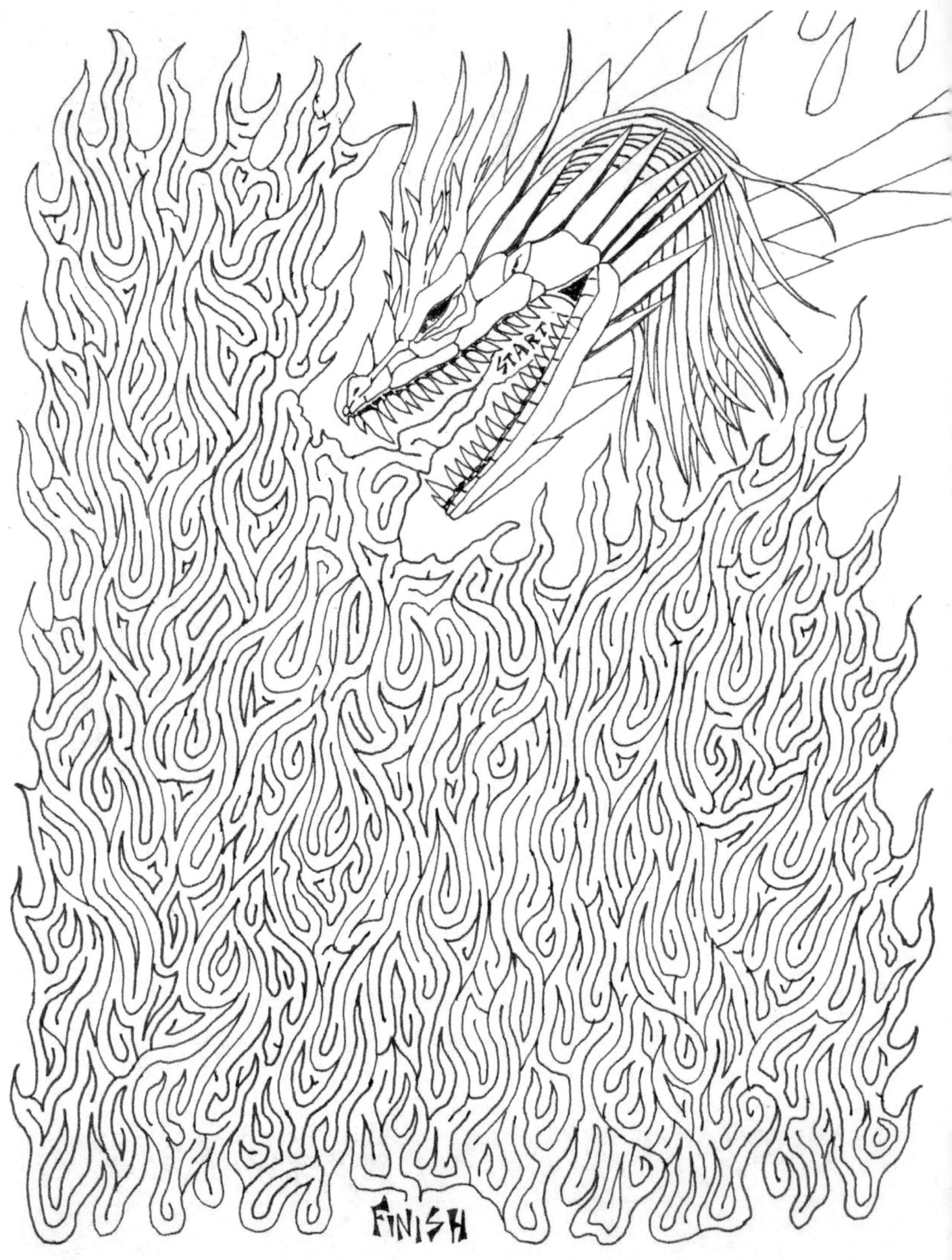

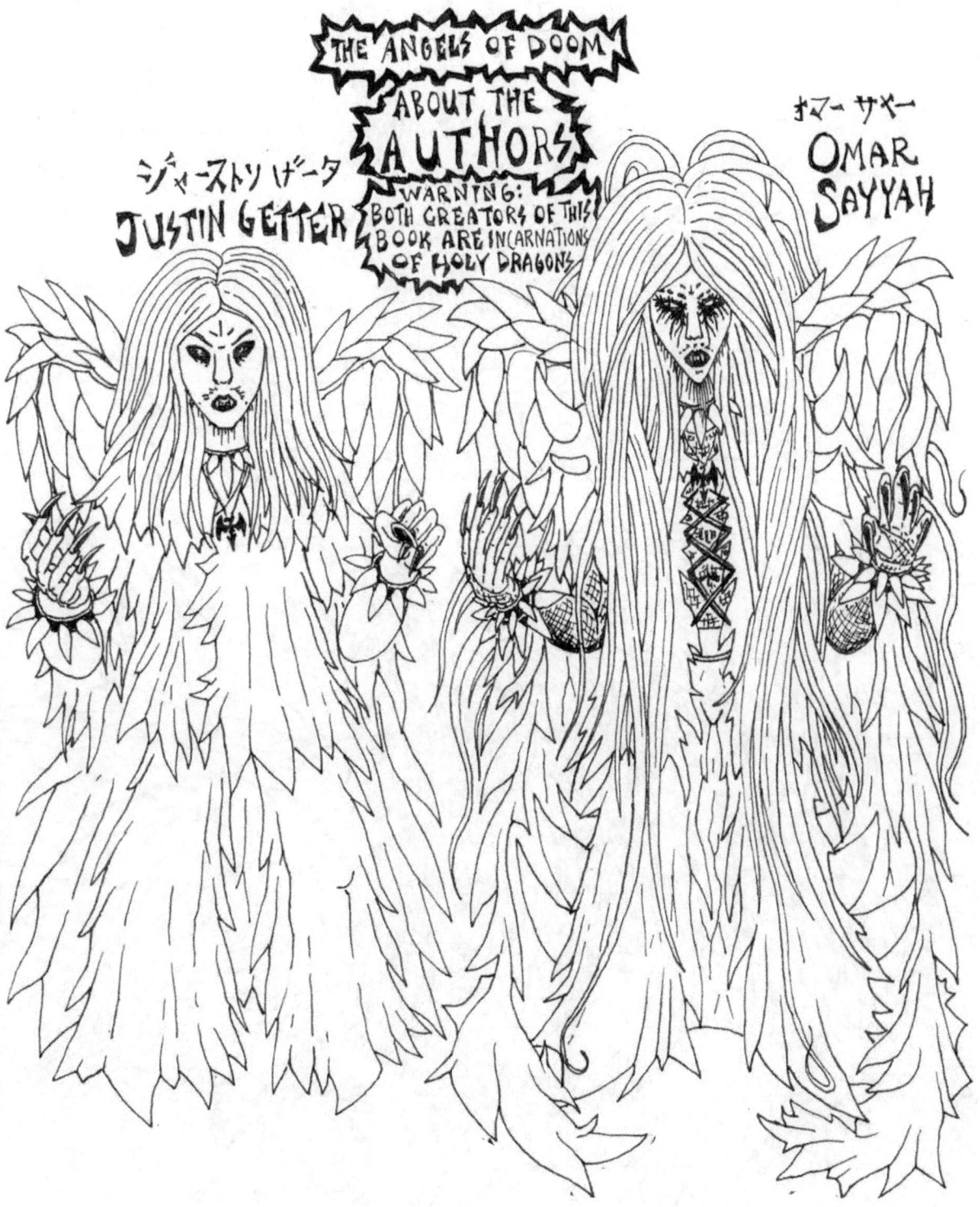

THE ANGELS OF DOOM
ABOUT THE AUTHORS
WARNING: BOTH CREATORS OF THIS BOOK ARE INCARNATIONS OF HOLY DRAGONS

ジャーストソ ゲータ
JUSTIN GETTER

オマー サヤー
OMAR SAYYAH

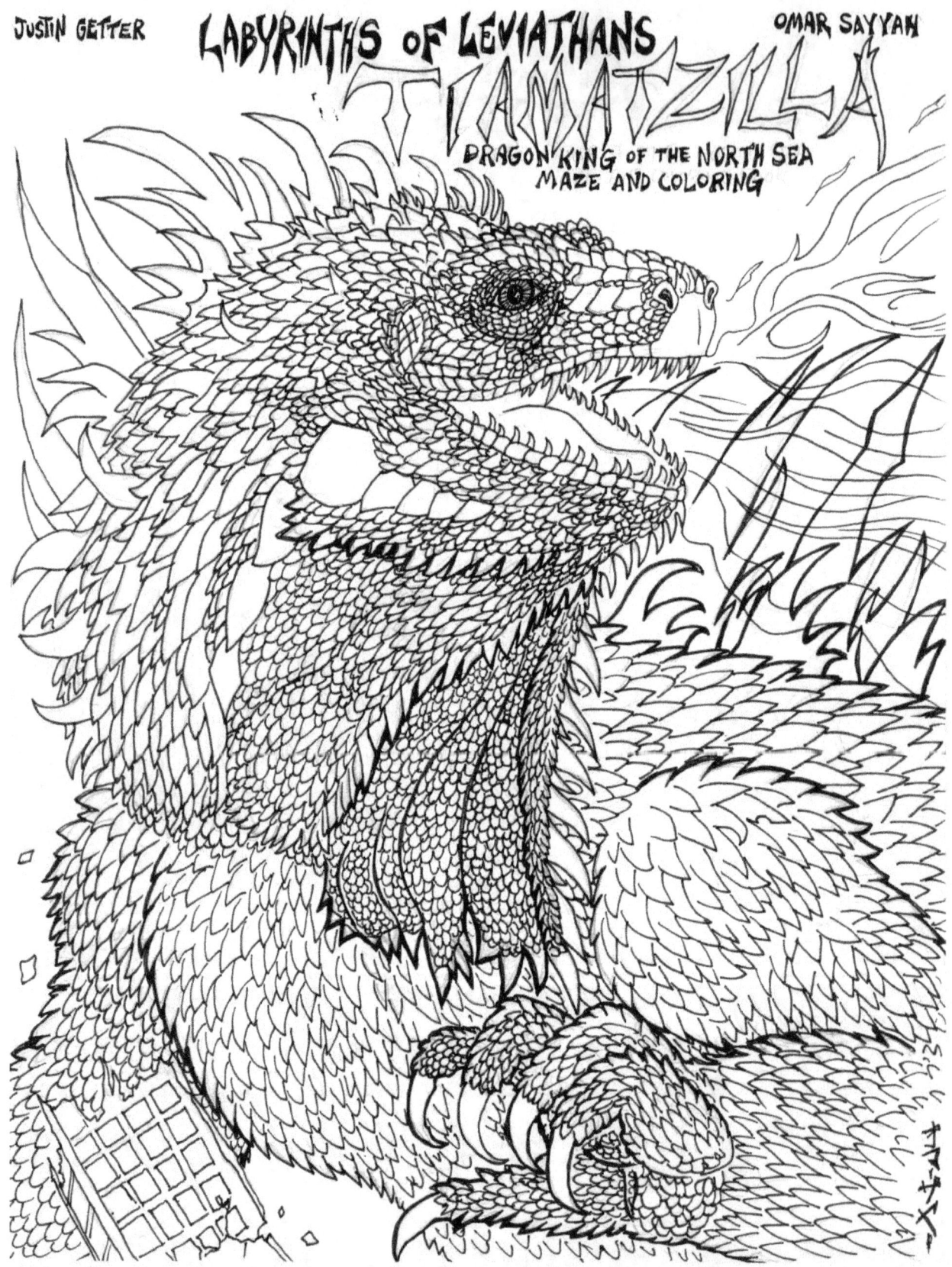

JUSTIN GETTER
LABYRINTHS OF LEVIATHANS
TIAMATZILLA
DRAGON KING OF THE NORTH SEA
MAZE AND COLORING
OMAR SAYYAH

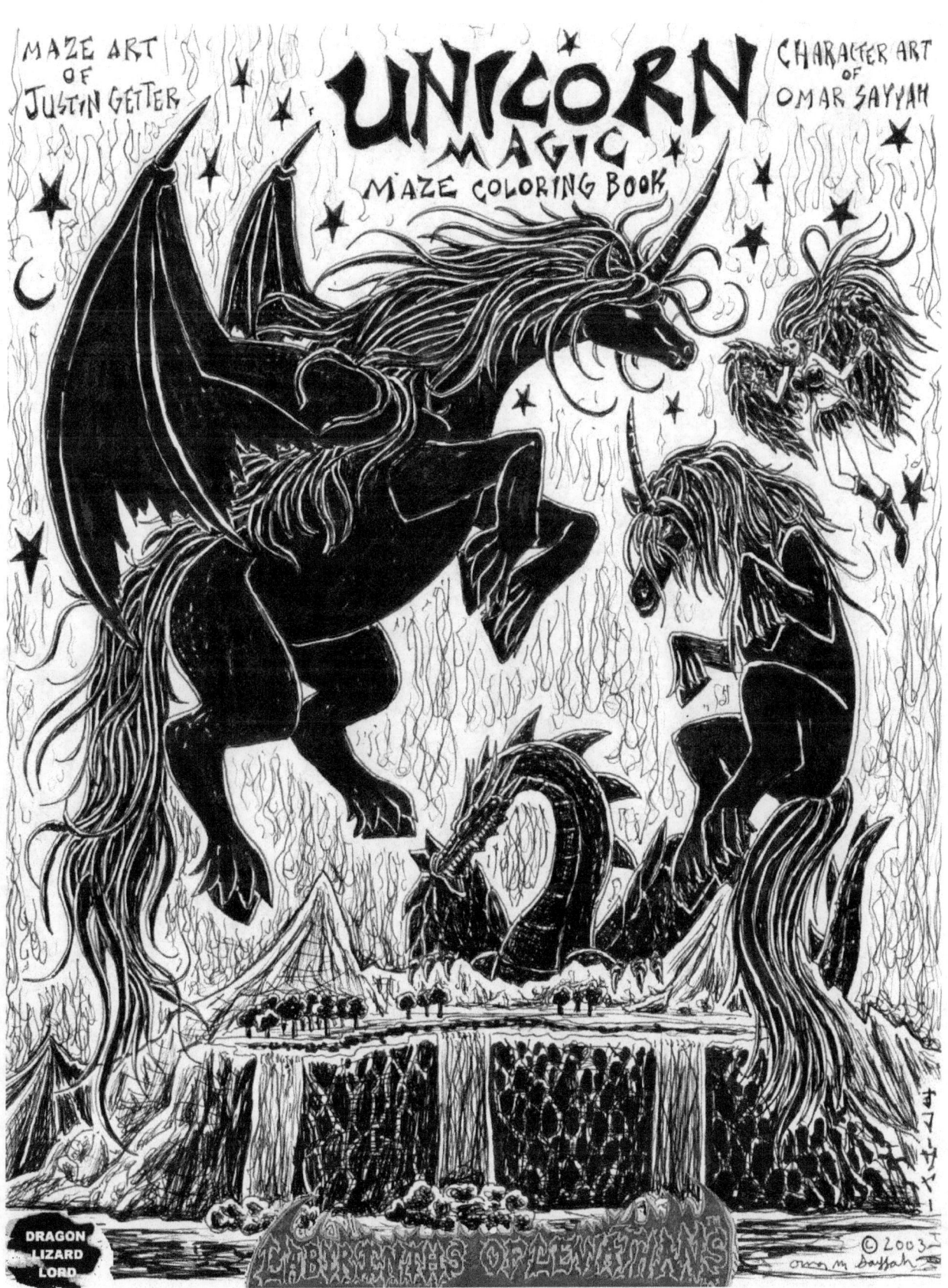

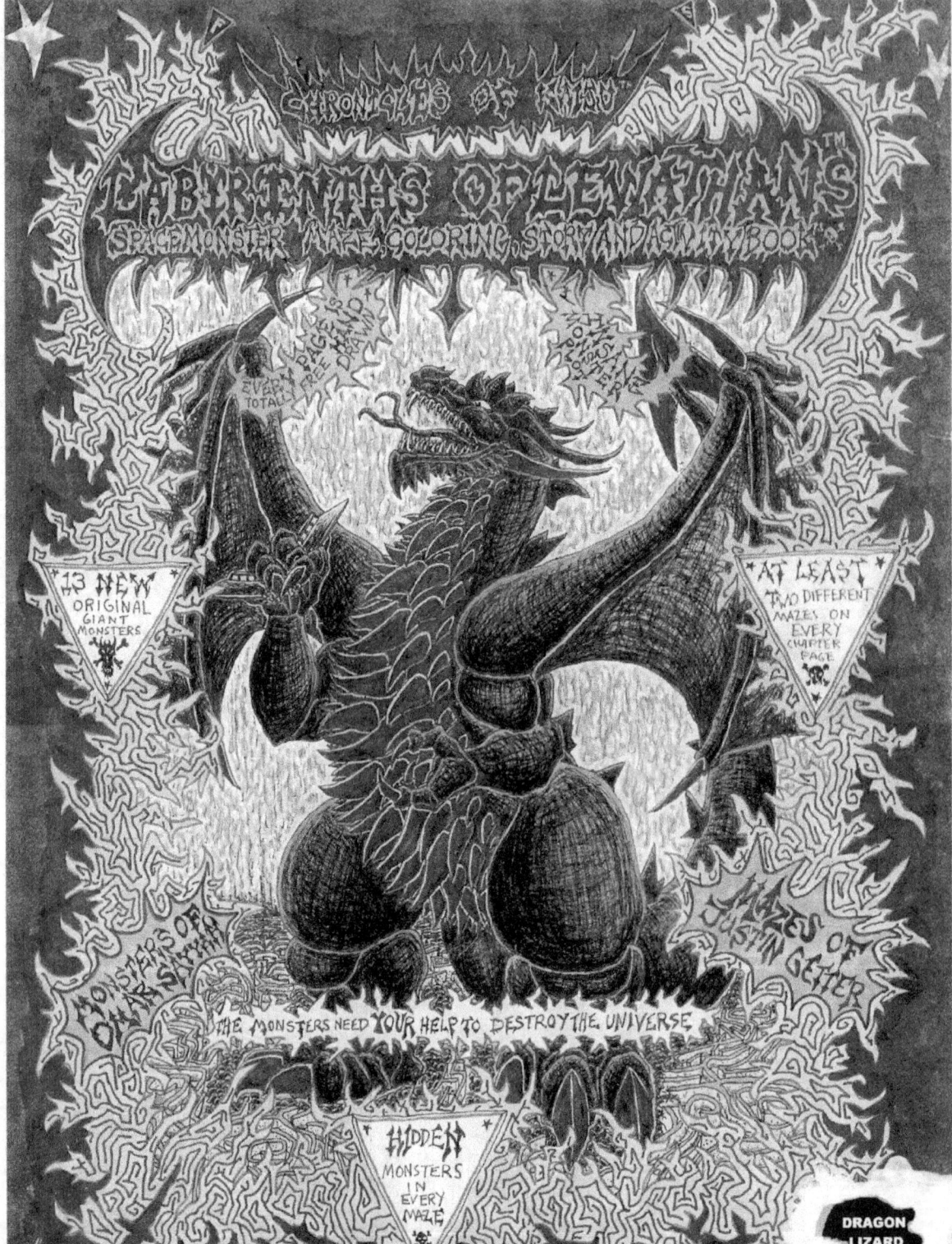

BY
OMAR SAYYAH

TIAMAT
VS
MARDUK

Dragon Legends

OMAR M. SAYYAH

TIAMATZILLA
VS.
THE KAIJU KONGS

DRAGON LEGENDS
BOOK 2